Ste. Genevieve
A Leisurely Stroll Through History

by Bill and Patti Naeger
and Mark L. Evans

First Published
July 1999

Second Printing
December 1999

ISBN 0-9676039-0-0

Published by
Merchant Street Publishing
123 Merchant Street
Ste. Genevieve, Missouri 63670
1-573-883-3221
Find us at www.stegenbook.com

Printed in the United States

Ste. Genevieve

A Leisurely Stroll Through History

by Bill and Patti Naeger
and Mark L. Evans

Contents

Section I

HISTORY..................................2-55

Begin your stroll here, through some of the highlights of Ste. Genevieve's past 250 years. Get to know Papa Vallé as he and his family made the transition from French to Spanish rule, then back to French before finally becoming Americans with the purchase of the Louisiana Territory. Meet some of the town's famed 19th Century characters such as John James Audubon and the renowned Senator Lewis Linn. Join Mayor Harry Petrequin and President Franklin D. Roosevelt at Ste. Genevieve's 1935 Bicentennial celebration. Finally, share the challenges that this historic mid-western town must face as it strives to blend its two centuries of history into the modern age of the new millenium.

Section II

ARCHITECTURE............. 56-131

Trace the architectural styles that give Ste. Genevieve its unique face. The rich legacy that the French left behind in their vertical log structures makes Ste. Genevieve uniquely significant in North American architecture. A number of structures remain standing which are representative of the Anglo-American period of the early 1800s. The German influx of the mid-1800s left its mark in a great many brick German vernacular and commercial structures which remain in daily use today. Not only museum houses, but structures in which the people of Ste. Genevieve live and work today, the town's architecture–one of its greatest assets–remains preserved and vibrant through two centuries.

KEY TO AUTHORS:

mle – Mark L. Evans

bn – Bill Naeger

psn – Patti Sexauer Naeger

*Except where noted, Sections I and II written by Mark L. Evans.

Contents

Section III

FLOODS..........................132-159

From its earliest history, the face of Ste. Genevieve has been influenced by the ever-present beck and call of the Mississippi River. Perhaps the most dramatic example of this was the gradual exodus in the late 1780s from the old town site in the river bottomland to the present location. Today the town continues to wrestle with the whims of the river. Join the town in its flood battle of 1993. The promise and completion of a federal levee won't come too soon for this flood-weary community.

Section IV

STE. GENEVIEVE LIVE...160-219

What every "outsider" should know to integrate into this tradition-rich community. From its food, to its music, to its lingo—discover the *joie de vivre* that the French passed onto the Germans and which remains alive today. Finally, end your stroll with a walk through the seasons.

Design, layout, graphics and typography by Bill Naeger.
Color photographs, except where noted, by Bill Naeger.
Edited by Bill and Patti Naeger.

*Except where noted, Sections III and IV written by Bill and Patti Naeger.

ACKNOWLEDGEMENTS I

Bill and I had both come up with the same basic idea in 1997. Each of us had decided to do a book on Ste. Genevieve. Mine would be a small, walking tour type book. There had also been talk of publishing some of my local history newspaper features in booklet form. Bill had been toying with the idea of doing a hardback "picture book" of Ste. Genevieve, featuring historic black and white shots and his own color photographs.

One late summer day in 1997, I entered Bill's shop and asked about the availability of old photos for my possible booklet. It was then that we learned of each other's ideas.

Within weeks a plan had begun to take shape. Abandoning our earlier individual plans, Bill and I decided to strike out together and do a "coffee table" book of our own.

Everyone has seemed to agree that Ste. Genevieve needed this type of book. Ste. Genevieve is a rare jewel, lending itself equally well to scholarly writing, folksy tales or breathtaking photography. We hope the reader will savor the aroma, sights and flavors of Ste. Genevieve within these pages and perhaps come back and visit in person.

Since this project began, numerous individuals and organizations have generously aided us in our quest to see this book become a reality. From the scholars who have previously studied and chronicled Ste. Genevieve, to the townspeople themselves, to our friends and family members, we have received nothing but kindness and support.

We gratefully acknowledge the help of many individuals. Dr. Carl J. Ekberg, noted colonial Ste. Genevieve scholar and author, was not only kind enough to give advice and to critique the text, but also agreed without hesitation to write the foreword. Gregory M. Franzwa, author of *The Story of Old Ste. Genevieve* and, in many ways, the man who put Ste. Genevieve on the map, has also been a most gracious and consistent supporter of the project. Other key figures to whom we are indebted include the legendary Charles F. Peterson, FAIA, the first architectual expert to "discover" Ste. Genevieve in the 1930s; Dr. Osmund Overby, without whose previous in-depth studies of Ste. Genevieve's historic structures and willingness to answer questions, critique text, and lend moral support, two such rank amateurs would never have considered doing a book dealing largely with architectural history; Dr. Charles Balesi, another noted author and French colonial expert, who has graced us with his advice and support; The National Society of The Colonial Dames in the State of Missouri, including State President Elizabeth Lewis, Bolduc House Museum Director Lorraine Stange and especially a dear supporter and lifelong friend of this community, Mrs. Margaret Mathews Jenks; the State Parks Division of the Department of Natural Resources, especially Jim Baker, site administrator of the Felix Valle State Historic Site and other local historic sites and his able staff; the Foundation for Restoration of Ste. Genevieve; the French Colonial Merchants Assocation; the Bed and Breakfast Association of Ste. Genevieve; the Ste. Genevieve Area Chamber of Commerce; The Great River Road Interpretive Center, especially the long-time queen of Ste. Genevieve tourism, Fran Ballinger; the Ste. Genevieve Visitors and Tourism Bureau, including Donna Card Charron and Bev Donze; *Les Amis,* including Elizabeth Gentry Sayad; *Alliance Français,* including Jane Robert; the Missouri Historical Society— especially the fine staff of its Skinker Boulevard research center; Timothy G. Conley, whose encouragement, support and advice have been priceless; fellow publisher/author Matt Chaney, whose support and practical advice have also been big boosts; my former employer Bob Burr and Jean Feld Rissover at *The Ste. Genevieve Herald,* who allowed us to reprint and/or cannibalize many of my previous Herald features in the book and who graciously turned their heads when five-minute trips to Bill's Photo Lab to "pick up film" occasionally turned into hour-long book production meetings; and finally, to the people of Ste. Genevieve themselves, who have helped keep the oldest permanent European settlement in Upper Louisiana attractive, historic, friendly, clean and safe enough to make visitors want to visit in person and through the pages of this book.

Mark Evans

ACKNOWLEDGEMENTS II

After twelve months of intensive work to prepare this book for press, I am gratefully sitting down to write one of its first pages in order to thank those who have been so helpful in bringing this work to completion.

First of all, thanks to the people of Ste. Genevieve who put their trust (not to mention their money) in us before there was ever a book in sight. Personally, had I had my way, we'd have never started advertising this book until it was near completion. But as my dear wife pointed out so adeptly, had we not collected money in advance, I would have never completed the project since there would have been no obligation to produce a product. About this she was absolutely right. Our house is full of unfinished projects and my brain is even fuller of projects I've not yet begun. So those of you who laid down your money in advance were instrumental to the completion of this book, and we thank you for it.

To those of you who lent photos and memorabilia from your personal collections for inclusion in the book, thanks for trusting us with your valued collections, especially the following individuals—Janet Abts, Pat Parker, Clarence Schwent, Joyce Bowen, Scott Basler, Kenny Cox, Becky Noce, Ken Barley, Jim and Carl Beyatte, Anna Thomure, Lorraine Uding, Lucille Eichenlaub, Millicent Sexauer, Norma Rottler, Fran Ballinger, Joel and Bev Donze, Francis Fay, Jr., George Wehner, Jack Myers, Harold Donze, Louise Wade, "Gump" Roth, Koetting's Foodway and "Took" Grobe(who passed away before the project was finished).

A special thanks to Betty Donze whose wonderful collection of Vince Dunker images give us a glimpse of Ste. Genevieve in the early 1900s. Lucille Basler allowed us to use several photos from her collection and assisted us with several items of research...thank you! Our appreciation goes to Barb Roth and Mae Elder at the Ozark Regional Library for allowing us to use the Bicentennial scrapbooks and also to the Ste.Genevieve Museum for access to the Joseph Oberle plates.

Artist and illustrator Brenda Gilliam's interest and critiques were a constant encouragement.

I thank the Ste. Genevieve Herald for allowing me access to retrieve the images I'd shot while employed there in 1982 and 1983. As it turned out, I was on staff there at a time of several significant events in Ste.Genevieve history—the Historic American Buildings Survey, the Bequette-Ribault House restoration, the winter flood of 1982, and the debate over demolition of the Kempf-Jaccard buildings—all topics dealt with in the book, so those images were invaluable.

I would like to thank Jean Feld Rissover for her helpful input regarding content and design.

A special thanks goes to Jim Baker of the Felix Valle State Historic Site whose timely research into the 19th Century architecture of Ste.Genevieve was invaluable as we dealt with that section of the book.

Thanks to Betty Valle Gegg who contributed to the book with her articles about the Project Pioneers and the Zell group from Germany. Her collaboration with Rick Williams in writing the "We Can Do This" account of the flood of 1993 for the Ste.Genevieve Herald served as a source of factual information as we compiled that section of the book.

To Dave Papin, I express my deep appreciation. As manager of Bill's Photo Lab, he held down the fort when, in the spring of 1998, I decided I needed to take a leave of absence from my primary business in order to complete this project. Thanks, Dave!

To all of you who lent moral and spiritual support, especially in the form of prayer. We all know this project would have never reached completion without God's blessing and help. I especially want to thank my prayer meeting buddies—Scott, Russ, Rob, Mark and David. A special thanks to my ten year old Xavier who never missed a night for the duration of the project in asking God's help for Dad's book.

And finally to my dear wife, Patricia, who came on board in the summer of 1998, giving up half of her gardening season to assist me at first with layout, then in an editorial capacity and later as a researcher and co-writer. Her contribution to the text has provided a much needed element of intimacy. Her hours spent pouring over HABS and land grant reports has made her a bit of an architectural historian in her own right.

Bill Naeger

The saint, Genevieve, lived in Paris in the fifth century. Through her lead and devotion to God, the city was spared many calamities.

When Attila and his army of Huns marched toward Paris, its citizens were preparing to abandon their city, but Genevieve encouraged them to avert the scourge through prayer and fasting.

In 1129, the "burning fever" plagued Paris and apparently it wasn't until the shrine of Saint Genevieve was carried in solemn procession that the sick were healed and the scourge lifted.

It is no wonder that the early French Catholic settlers in the Illinois country elected to name their new settlement after such a faithful guardian.

This painting, high on the wall in Ste. Genevieve Catholic Church, shows the saint keeping prayerful vigil over her beloved town.

PREFACE

During the "kick off" open house for this book in January, 1998, a young skateboarder happened in off the street for some of the free refreshments and asked my wife, Patti, "What's going on here, anyway?" When informed that it was a reception for a forthcoming book about Ste.Genevieve, he crinkled his face, "A book about Ste.Genevieve? How boring!" She answered, "Oh, don't you think Ste.Genevieve is interesting?" To which he responded, "No. Well…(thoughtful pause) … maybe…(thoughtful pause)…Jour de Fete…and the flood—that was fun," then added, "but how could anyone write a whole book." At this, my amused wife produced a copy of Carl Ekberg's voluminous work *Colonial Ste.Genevieve: An Adventure on the Mississippi Frontier* and explained that this expert work only covered the first 50-75 years of Ste.Genevieve's history. She then introduced the wide-eyed youngster to the author.

Having grown up in Ste. Genevieve, I could have empathized with the young man's lack of enthusiasm (he might call it boredom) over what there *isn't* to do in Ste.Genevieve or his lack of appreciation for the history of which he is a part. Drawing upon what little knowledge I had of the subject when composing an "our town" essay in Mrs. Miller's sixth grade history class, I, too, was only vaguely aware of my presence in this mecca of French colonial history.

I can say, though, that as an adolescent strolling the streets of Ste.Genevieve at night when everything was quiet, I was aware of something beyond the present. The "feel" of Ste.Genevieve inspired my imagination. Whether walking through Memorial Cemetery on a moonlit night or Bill Hoffman's junkyard after a newfallen snow or standing in the nave of Ste.Genevieve Catholic Church with only the shadows cast by devotional candles dancing on the vaulted ceiling — Ste.Genevieve's aura not only sent chills up my spine, but transported me to another time as well.

Looking back now, I realize that those experiences and the skills I developed along the way have brought me to an appreciation for my home town and the ability to share it with you.

For me, today, it's what there *isn't* to do in Ste.Genevieve that appeals to me most. It's a haven from the bustling life in the fast lane of the rest of the world. I'm one who would prefer to see Ste.Genevieve remain undiscovered for fear it may lose its essentially "laid back" atmosphere. Fu-*tourist*-ically speaking, Ste.Genevieve can remain a "sleeper" as far as I am concerned.

But it won't.

So you may ask, "Why am I involved in a book that exposes this treasure to the outside world?"

In hopes that you might see this town through my eyes and that together we may preserve the quintessential* Ste.Genevieve.

Whether you do it first hand or let your fingers do the walking through the pages of this book, I hope you enjoy your stroll.

*quintessence: *the essence of a thing in its purest and most concentrated form*

FOREWORD

It is a well-known, but still arresting, fact that historic Ste.Genevieve has been more appreciated by outsiders than by Ste.Genevievens themselves. Familiarity has surely not bred contempt, but it has generated a certain diffidence and complacency about the cultural significance of the town. Many local folks tend to be more concerned with the success of the Ste.Genevieve and Valle High School football teams (And very good teams they are!) than they are with the historical and architectural treasures that surround them. The most recent books about Ste.Genevieve, Gregory M. Franzwa's *The Story of Old Ste.Genevieve* and my own *Colonial Ste.Genevieve: An Adventure on the Mississippi Frontier,* were written by rank outsiders with neither roots nor residences in the community. And the "discoverer" in the 1930s of Ste.Genevieve's architectural legacy, Charles E. Peterson, was a Minnesotan employed by the National Park Service in St. Louis.

All this is now changed with the appearance of *Ste.Genevieve: A Leisurely Stroll Through History,* with text by Mark L. Evans and Bill and Patti Naeger and photographs by Bill Naeger. These authors are not only residents of Ste.Genevieve, they also have ancient ancestral roots in the community. It is fitting that their forebears were French and German, for these particular ethnic groups have made deep and enduring cultural contributions to Ste.Genevieve. This is apparent whether one is admiring the town's unique collection of French colonial log houses or savoring the delicacy of Oberle's German sausages.

The French roots obviously run deepest. Mark's Aubuchon ancestors immigrated to Canada in 1644—during the era of King Louis XIII, Cardinal Richelieu and the Three Musketeers. Antoine Aubuchon, born in Montreal in 1703, moved to the Mississippi Valley during the early 1730s, married in Kaskaskia in 1739, and became one of Ste.Genevieve's original in-

habitants. That is, Antoine was a resident of Ste.Genevieve at the earliest date that one can identify a town of that name, and he is listed as a head of household on the 1752 French census of the "Vilage de Ste. Junnevieve." Book-learning was not a strong suit of Major Jean-Jacques Macarty, the French commandant of Fort de Chartres on the east side of the Mississippi River who drafted this census.

Bill's ancestors—led by his great-great-grandfather, Mathias Neger, arrived in the Ste.Genevieve area from the Offenburg region of western Germany in 1846, having sailed from Havre on the American passenger ship *Monument.* This was an early date for the arrival of German immigrants, the large influx of which did not begin until after the political upheavals that wracked Germany during the revolutions of 1848. So, as Mark's ancestors were among the earliest French settlers in the town, Bill's were among the earliest Germans. Eighteenth-century Ste.Genevieve was purely Roman Catholic in faith, and the nineteenth-century town was heavily so despite the arrival of some Anglo-American Protestants. Most Germans who immigrated to the Ste.Genevieve region during the mid-nineteenth century were also Catholics and as such Bill's ancestors were able to integrate successfully and comfortably into the local community.

Patti's ancestors, too, were part of the German influx of the mid-1800s. Her great-great-grandfather George Sexauer I from Emidiga-baden and her great-grandfather Christian Baum from Lauchroden were among the original trustees of the German Lutheran Evangelical Church—Kreuz Kirche—located at the southwestern corner of Market and Second Streets.

Now, for the book that follows. Never before has anyone contrived to integrate an historical narrative of Ste.Genevieve with a high-style photographic record of the town's important historic sites. This has been handsomely accomplished thanks to the successful collaboration of the authors—Mark, Bill and Patti. Ste. Genevieve is perfectly suited for this collaborative approach because the town is blessed with both a uniquely interesting history and a particularly photogenic character in its historic buildings and landscapes.

This volume argues forcefully that Ste. Genevieve is most emphatically not a miniature Midwestern Williamsburg. Unlike the restored capitol of colonial Virginia, Ste.Genevieve is not a restoration project; it is not a contrived time capsule, but rather a living, evolving community that happens to possess multitudinous historical treasures. On the one hand this means that some historic buildings are lost; on the other it means that there is a vibrancy that cannot be duplicated in famous restoration projects such as Williamsburg or Fortress Louisbourg. Where else on a hot Midwestern day may one have a beer in a brick tavern that survived the New Madrid earthquakes of 1811-12, or enjoy an ice cream in an antebellum Federal style building that has been a commercial property for more than 150 years? In their particular wisdom, bred of deep roots and unabashed parochial loyalties, the citizens of Ste.Genevieve have made a vital, though seldom articulated, decision: Don't try to compete with the East Coast, for we've got something better right here in our own town.

Colonial Ste.Genevieve, the Ste.Genevieve that existed before Thomas Jefferson had ever heard of Louisiana and before Lewis and Clark had ever set eyes on the trans-Mississippian West, naturally occupies a privileged place in this book. As noted in the text, this town, remarkably, possesses more French-built buildings than New Orleans. Take a moment to let that sink in! But in keeping with the premise that it is the entire fabric of the community, across the centuries and through changing tastes and fashions, that provides Ste.Genevieve with its peculiar charm, the Naegers and Evans have bitten off the whole thing—from the founding of the town in mid-eighteenth century to the flood of 1993. Therefore, the reader will be delighted to find in these pages not only descriptions and photos of French colonial buildings, but also captivating coverage of an entire gamut of nineteenth-century architectural styles—early American Federal, German brick, Italianate, Second Empire, Gothic revival, and so forth. And one will also find the way in which the citizens of the town have dealt with great floods from that of 1785 to the end of the twentieth century.

This book about Ste.Genevieve's history is also a history of how history has been construed in the town. Centennial celebrations are a perennial favorite of small-town Americans, and in 1885 the citizens of Ste.Genevieve celebrated the founding of the New Town that occurred after the great flood of 1785. The punishingly hot temperatures that July day were perhaps a form of penance for having selected an inaccurate date, for the move to the

New Town, though prompted by the 1785 flood, was not consummated until 1793. But as the great American historian Carl Becker once observed: It's not important that a history be complete, or even completely true; but it is essential that it be useful. And one of the enduring, and endearing, characteristics of Ste. Genevievens since the town's founding has been a pragmatism first carried to the western shore of the Mississippi by settlers of French-Canadian peasant stock. Jean-Baptiste Vallé was born a Frenchman, became a Spaniard, then became French once again, before finally becoming a citizen of Thomas Jefferson's American republic, and being the eminently practical person that he was, had no trouble swearing unreserved fidelity to each of these regimes in turn without batting an eye—or altering his profound loyalty to his town—i.e. Ste. Genevieve. This sense of the practical is so powerful that it quickly seizes "foreigners" who come to settle down in the community. In 1985, for example, Bernie Schram—who, having lived in the town a mere twenty-five years and having made myriad contributions to the community, was still an outsider—made the sly observation that if 1985 was not necessarily the correct date for celebrating Ste. Genevieve's two-hundred-and-fiftieth anniversary, it most certainly was the correct date for celebrating the fiftieth anniversary of the bicentennial celebration that had transpired in 1935. Quite true—and very pragmatic.

The 1885 centennial celebration was a bit of a flop—weather too hot, speeches too long, and beer too abundant; feting the founding of a French colonial town provoked an extravagant thirst in the numerous citizens with German roots. The bicentennial celebration in 1935 (Don't be confused. Remember, 1885 was the centennial celebration of the establishment of the New Town of Ste. Genevieve.) was a good deal more successful. It was not only better organized and better orchestrated, the celebration provided an occasion to be less de-pressed by the Great Depression of the thirties—and stimulated some serious thinking about how informed tourism might generate revenues for the community. The bicentennial of 1935 having placed historic Ste. Genevieve on the map, soon Charles Peterson persuaded a pump-priming federal government to create the Historic American Buildings Survey (HABS). Documenting Ste. Genevieve's historic structures was one of the first projects of the survey's young, heretofore unemployed, architects. The community now has high hopes that this same federal government will provide the wherewithal to build a levee and safeguard the town's historic treasures from the wrathful Father of Waters. Write your congressman! The preservation of historic Ste. Genevieve might serve to immortalize his memory.

The preceding paragraphs are merely a foretaste of the delights that await the reader of this elegant book. This volume is not intended to be read from cover to cover in one or two sittings. Rather, it is meant to be had at the ready on the coffee table, whenever one is demoralized by the tawdry spectacle of strip malls, gambling casinos, fast-food joints, and soap operas. Then open this book and retire to the gallery of the Bolduc House, the garden of the Jean-Baptiste Vallé House, the courtyard of the Mammy Shaw House, or the sanctuary of the Ste. Genevieve parish church. This experience will give one pause to ponder over the content and direction of American civilization in the late twentieth century.

Dr. Carl J. Ekberg

The Great River Road Interpretive Center, opens for another day,
orienting visitors to the wealth of history which Ste. Genevieve has to offer.

The fertile bottomland on the west bank of the Mississippi River held the promise of a richer life for the early settlers.

INTRODUCTION

Roaring unchecked from what is now Minnesota, to the Gulf of Mexico, the mighty river did more than offer transportation, irrigation and constant danger to Indians and European explorers. The Mississippi also served as a boundary. To its east lay the known colonial world, already beginning to fill with pioneer families eager to hack out a better existence. To its west roamed the mighty Osage Indians and other tribes, as well as a seemingly inexhaustible supply of wild game and towering timber.

For generations of American settlers, the banks of the Mississippi marked the jumping off point from the relative security of the East, into the untamed frontier.

Whatever the exact year farmers from Kaskaskia and other locations on the east bank crossed over and built the first log homes of Ste. Genevieve, a huge foothold was secured. Life on the west of the mighty river would prove to be taxing. The little village of Ste. Genevieve, however, would survive, becoming the first permanent white settlement west of the river in Upper Louisiana and one of the oldest permanent towns in the Midwest.

The town made one concession to the roaring river. During the late 1780s and early 1790s the villagers reluctantly abandoned their original town on the alluvial plain along *le grand champ,* "the Big Field," where their crops grew in abundance when not inundated by flood water. Regular flooding and the erosion of the riverbank—as well as the likely exhaustion of available land—led to the gradual move. The hardy French settlers, by now under Spanish rule, moved about two miles uphill, between the forks of the North and South Gabouri Creeks. The new settlement was first called *les petites côtes,* "the little hills." This would be the last concession the determined Frenchmen would make to "Old Man River," surviving more than 200 years and numerous floods, as well as years of threats of Indian and "foreign" attack and the hardships of frontier life.

Today Ste. Genevieve remains remarkably intact. Perhaps Lorraine Stange, long-time manager of the restored circa 1793 Louis Bolduc House, said it best. "People always tell me Ste. Genevieve could be another Williamsburg (Va.). I always say 'Why would we want to be? What we have here is real.'"

Stange has hit the square wooden peg on the head. Ste. Genevieve colonial structures are just that—structures built while the town was a royal colony. There are no historical reproductions in Ste. Genevieve—save one stone kitchen built in the 1950s. Ste. Genevieve is a living, working piece of North American history.

Gregory M. Franzwa, author of *The Story of Old Ste. Genevieve,* the most popular book ever written on the old town, also had it pegged. "Here is what happens when nothing happens for a couple of centuries," he wrote on the back cover of his book, now in its sixth printing, "no slums, no fires, no urban renewal projects, no sprawling shopping centers. The residue is a natural structural legacy otherwise unknown in America."

This is Ste. Genevieve—at least one side of her. "The Mother City of the West," as her promoters called her at the time of her 1935 bicentennial celebration, combines rich colonial history, unique historical architecture, a surviving slice of French colonial culture and all the charm of a small, friendly, extremely attractive Midwestern town.

This is surprising, spellbinding Ste. Genevieve. Enjoy a leisurely stroll through history along her streets and in these pages.

HISTORY
Kaskaskia – *The Cradle of Ste. Genevieve*

Kaskaskia can legitimately be called the cradle of Ste. Genevieve. By and large the ancestors of Ste. Genevieve's French population migrated from France to Canada and from there to the river town of Kaskaskia. The two historic towns hold many things in common.

Like Ste. Genevieve, Kaskaskia existed because of the river. And like her neighbor to the west, the river has often turned brutally against her, forcing her to struggle with dogged determination to survive. Likely founded in 1703, the village was inhabited by Jesuit priests and fur traders in the early days. The population had soared to six hundred or more by 1767.

The importance of Kaskaskia, which had become "the main source of food supply for New Orleans and its dependent military outposts," according to Dr. Gerald W. Ellis, in his "A Study of Kaskaskia, Illinois," was illustrated in 1741, when King Louis XV of France gave the legendary Kaskaskia Bell to the town, for the Church of the Immaculate Conception.

The silver and bronze bell, with the inscription *"Pour L'église des Illinois par les soins du Roi d'autre l'eau,"* (for the church of Illinois by the gift of the King from across the water."), was shipped from France, via New Orleans. The arduous journey took two years. Men were said to walk along the bank of the Mississippi, pulling the raft that carried the 650-pound bell with hand lines. The bell, eleven years older then the Liberty Bell, rang on July 4, 1778, when George Rogers Clark took over Kaskaskia for the American revolutionaries. It was the first bell chime to be heard west of the Alleghenies and also rang long and loud when the Marquis de LaFayette visited Kaskaskia in 1825. The bell was placed in the newly-completed Immaculate Conception Church in 1843. It was retired in 1874, when a hairline crack was discovered. It sat on the floor of the church until 1948, when the current shrine (which includes a Roscoe Misselhorn painting of the old village of Kaskaskia) was built.

A British possession after the close of the French and Indian War in 1763, the town became a melting pot of society. European and American settlers began to move in and the Kaskaskia Indians moved out, as the early 1800s progressed. In 1809 Kaskaskia became the capital of the Illinois Territory and in 1818, the first capital of the new state of Illinois. The population, according to some researchers, came close to 1,000 during those days.

The capital moved to Vandalia in 1820, however, and in 1848 the Randolph County seat moved to Chester from Kaskaskia, which had been inundated badly in the 1844 (as well as 1785) flood. "The population decreased until Kaskaskia became a sleepy rural community, with frequent flooding," Ellis wrote.

By the 1870s, the community's future looked grave, as the Mississippi continued eating away the buffer between itself and the Kaskaskia River. By the spring of 1881 disaster appeared to be at hand. The "narrows," or strip of land between the two rivers, had been cut to only 500 feet by early 1881. The most important date in Kaskaskia history was April 18, 1881. The two rivers finally met, eating away the final section of "narrows."

The Mississippi, seemingly tired of its old course, which swung a loop to the west, curving past St. Mary, Mo., forged through the new rift and eventually took over the old Kaskaskia channel. "Within a few days steamships were passing through the new channel with soundings of 66 feet," Ellis noted. In the process of taking over the Kaskaskia River channel, the Mississippi eventually buried the ancient village of Kaskaskia. According to Emily Lyons of the Randolph County Historical Society, Kaskaskia residents made numerous appeals for help to the Corps of Engineers and politicians during the 1880s. All fell on deaf ears and the mighty river cut deeper and deeper into the bank, until the long-feared disaster was finally at hand in the 1890s.

As the ground was eroded away, hundred-year-old French Creole homes and any other structures left behind, collapsed and fell into the swirling waters. Fragments of the colonial village are presumably still preserved beneath the silt, and the current path of the river. A handful of buildings were taken down and rebuilt on the new island, including the Immaculate Conception Church—moved between 1891 and 1894.

Enough of the old Mississippi River channel remained to make Kaskaskia an island. The incorporated village of Kaskaskia was laid out in the center of the new island by the same name. This actually boosted the Kaskaskia population for a few years, with the abundance of new, rich (and cheap) farm land on the island. By some sources, the population peaked at more than 1,200 people in the early 1890s. With more non-resident farmers owning much of the island, population began to gradually decrease in the 1900s, to about 300 as the 1970s began.

The island was believed to be protected by a federal levee—at least 10,000 of the approximately 14,000 acres of the island. Although flood stage had been reached one hundred and nine times in one hundred years, flood water had never reached the interior of the island as the spring of 1973 arrived.

Heavy snowfall in the winter of 1972-73 set the stage for the disaster that befell the island in 1973. The river was above the Chester flood gauge for a whopping ninety-seven consecutive days, beginning March 5, with a record crest of 43.32 feet recorded April 30. The long-dreaded levee failure finally occurred on April 27. Water topped the levee near Dozaville and ate great hunks of it, washing across the island with frightening ferocity. According to Ellis, seventy-eight of 111 buildings on the island were destroyed and all suffered considerable damage. Water was 19 feet deep in some locations and eight feet deep inside the Immaculate Conception sanctuary.

Disaster was barely staved off during the winter flood of 1982-83, as 60,000 sandbags helped hold the levee. It could not be avoided in 1993, when another levee failure led to a similar scenario as 1973. Once again the entire island lay beneath several feet of water, the Kaskaskia Bell and Church of the Immaculate Conception suffering heavy damages.

Once again, though, the island has fought back. The church parish successfully opposed an archdiocese move to close the church. The historic structure was restored and some seventy-five residents returned by the fall of 1998 to live on the island.

The Fort Kaskaskia overlook in Illlinois offers a view of the Mississippi River at the site of the old town of Kaskaskia.

Indian mounds are silhouetted against the reflection of a dawning sky in the floodwaters of a swollen Mississippi River. Located near the original town site in the Big Fields south of present-day Ste. Genevieve, the mounds remain a monument to a pre-white culture. Flooding was not uncommon two centuries ago and was responsible, in part, for the eventual move of the town to its present location.

The Birth of a New French Settlement

Historians have debated the actual founding date of Ste. Genevieve for more than a century. The best scholarly sources now place the founding around 1749, rather than the traditional 1735 date, the anniversary of which is still celebrated. The later date certainly takes nothing away from the significance of colonial Ste. Genevieve. As Mayor Harry J. Petrequin put it in a speech over KMOX radio prior to the town's bicentennial celebration in 1935, "Ste Genevieve is truly a Mother City of this vast territory...It was here that the ember of civilization in the District of (Upper) Louisiana was kept alive until it could be taken up by other hands and carried on over the mountains and plains of our western states."

Ste. Genevieve was not—as it long claimed—the first permanent white settlement west of the Mississippi. It is the oldest surviving town in Upper Louisiana, though, and unarguably is Missouri's oldest permanent settlement. Ste.Genevieve, as Petrequin said in the same speech, is "a rich, old tapestry of history." That history began nearly 250 years ago.

A few individual families could conceivably have lived on or near the future site of Ste. Genevieve in the 1730s, but the town was not recognized as an entity until mid-century. This has been firmly established by Dr. Carl J. Ekberg, the most noted scholar on colonial Ste. Genevieve.

The town was definitely established by 1750, though. One of the earliest written documents from Ste.Genevieve is a 1752 census, taken by Major Jean-Jacques Macarty, commandant of nearby Fort de Chartres. It can be interpreted as listing either twenty-three or twenty-five residents, including slaves, with eight heads of household. The clear leader of the young community was André Deguire *dit* LaRose, who would soon become captain of the militia, despite being well into his sixties.

Papa Vallé

About 1754 an important family made its move to Ste. Genevieve. François Vallé, who had earlier immigrated from Quebec to Kaskaskia, crossed the river with his wife, the former Marianne Billeron. By 1760, Vallé had replaced the aging Deguire as militia captain and also held the title *lieutenant particulier*. As Ekberg has noted, Vallé seemingly could read and write (having supposedly been taught by his wife), while Deguire was illiterate. This, as well as Deguire's age, may have been a factor in Vallé taking over the position. Although Spanish archives give no hint to Vallé holding the title "commandant," as has been passed down in Ste. Genevieve lore, his *lieutenant particulier* title gave him more or less the responsibilities of a civil commandant or civil judge.

One of the legendary characters in Ste. Genevieve history, François Vallé was commonly known as "Papa" Vallé. Although his duties forced him to toss a few troublemakers into the "calaboose," as the local jail was always known, he seemed to be a beloved figure in the town's colonial era.

He was no one's fool, either. When the Spanish finally arrived in August, 1767—four years after officially winning the Louisiana Territory from Spain in the Seven Year's War, Vallé was quick to make his mark. He fed and apparently housed Francisco Riu, commander of the Spanish force. He did the same three years later for Don Pedro Piernas, the new lieutenant governor of the Louisiana Territory, when he passed through Ste. Genevieve on his way to St. Louis.

An astute politician (as his sons would also prove to be), Vallé knew when to pour on the charm and understood enough rudimental psychology to paint any personal enemies he gathered

as enemies of the Spanish crown when communicating with the Spanish hierarchy. As a result, Vallé maintained his title and his place of prominence in the community the rest of his life.

One person Vallé did not get along with was the bizarre Capuchin friar, Father Hilaire de Geneveaux, Ste. Genevieve pastor from 1773–1777. Father Hilaire was one of the most eccentric characters in the town's early history. The priest was in the center of controversy his entire time in Ste. Genevieve. His escapades began with demanding a ten percent tithe from his parishoners rather than the one twenty-sixth percent to which they were accustomed and insisting on his own domestic servant. He was accused of not delivering sermons, failing to instruct the youth in the ways of the faith, and refusing to give Extreme Unction to one of Vallé's dying black slaves.

The most famous incident occurred in the summer of 1775, when Vallé's church pew disappeared, during the height of Hilaire's feud with Vallé (and, indeed, most of the congregation). It was later found, smashed to pieces behind the rectory. After three years of complaining to the Spanish authorities, the parishioners finally gave Hilaire the bum's rush in 1777. Those who fought the Vallé family generally didn't stay in Ste. Genevieve long.

"Code Noir" on the French Frontier

Although it has not often been recognized, the role African-Americans and Native Americans played in the forming and sustaining of colonial Ste. Genevieve was monumental.

Obviously, slave labor helped the small village carve out a swatch along the wild Mississippi and gain a foothold. Dr. Carl J. Ekberg believes that Catholic missionaries may have brought the first slaves to the Illinois Country as early as 1719. The first Ste. Genevieve census, taken in 1752, mentions two adult slaves and a number of slave children.

By the time the town was firmly in place (although the river bank was not), black and Indian slavery was an important part of the colonists' way of life. The 1773 census showed 276 blacks, out of 676 total residents (41 percent). By 1800 the total population had risen to 1,163 and the black and mulatto slave population to 350.

"The heretofore neglected black people of colonial Ste. Genevieve deserve study," Ekberg wrote in his Colonial Ste. Genevieve, "not only because they made up a significant segment of the town's population but because their history sheds new light on the history of the entire town and its people."

The black-white cohabitation of Ste. Genevieve has been interesting from the beginning. It has always been a town where a few black families, meeting certain behavioral criteria, could live and work basically as equal participants in the life of the community. Yet few black families have come and stayed long.

The vertical log buildings on St. Mary Road were largely built by the sweat of black slaves. So were most of the surviving colonial structures of the new town. The power elite of old Ste. Genevieve (the Vallés, Louis Bolduc and later St. Gemme Beauvais and Janis) were large slave owners. Local Indians also found their way into slavery.

The French and Spanish colonial brand of slavery, as Ekberg has detailed, was much different from slavery in the South and Southeast.

Although slavery was slavery, the French colonial version seemed a bit more humanitarian and was apparently not based on ideas of racial superiority. Slavery had existed since Biblical times and was considered a way of life to all but a few enlightened thinkers of the day. The renowned French "Black Code" or Code Noir, recognized slaves as humans and set forth 55 articles insisting on proper treatment of slaves. While this was probably more motivated by economics than tender feelings, it nevertheless provided a bearable life for the slaves. While slave revolts were frequent in Lower Louisiana, no real threat of one ever surfaced in Upper Louisiana.

One thing that may have helped was the proverbial light at the end of the tunnel. In French and Spanish America, slaves were free to take jobs for hire during their free time. One could then literally buy his/her own freedom. Many did so.

By all appearances (and not enough documentation exists to form a really clear picture), former slaves seem to have been accepted as equal members of the community.

While ordinances were passed at various times, outlawing slaves from congregating and drinking, many slaves seem to have earned a great degree of trust from their masters. François and Jean Baptiste Vallé alarmed some of the more aristocratic newcomers by allowing their slaves to carry firearms. Justifying their actions, the Vallés noted that the slaves needed protection from "tigres" and other wild animals.

According to Ekberg, the French Creoles who had migrated from France to Canada and then to Kaskaskia, before crossing the river to Ste. Genevieve, had developed a remarkably non-racist mentality.

The River Runs Wild

In retrospect, the Creole settlers—those born in North America of French ancestry—probably had not picked the best location to settle in the first place. Erosion was a problem from early on. Floods, the threat of harrassment or attack from across the river and a lack of available land for house lots became increasingly troublesome as the eighteenth century wound down. These factors eventually led to the demise of the old settlement.

According to Ekberg, the first records of new land being requested and granted date to the spring of 1771. One of four requests made that spring specifically addressed erosion as the problem.

By the end of the decade the river was becoming an increasingly serious problem. Nearly 700 people (including children and slaves) were jammed together in the mosquito-infested alluvial plain. Floods wiped out crops two of every five years and were beginning to direct their vengeance toward the vertical log homes of the settlers as well. More and more east bank *habitants* were wishing to escape English rule and come to the area, but available land was running out. At the same time, the river apparently was beginning to make much more serious inroads into the bank, causing a number of people to move their homes. Professor Susan Flader of the University of Missouri has even speculated that there were, in essence, two "old" townsites. After the terrible flood of 1777, she believes, the church and a number of homes were moved out of the original horizontal line along the river bank and bunched into the center of the site. An exhaustive archaeological dig of the old townsite is the only thing that can possibly suggest answers to many baffling questions about the original town.

Of course the single most enduring image of the Old Town is that of *L'année des grandes eaux*, "the Year of the Great Waters." In the spring of 1785 the mighty river turned savage, inundating the village with a flood that is still legend more than two centuries later. The image is still vivid and lifelike of Auguste Chouteau's barges paddling into the scene of submerged houses and tying up to a chimney. While some youthful boatmen dove into the deep water, others simply stared, dumb-founded, as the tips of thatch roofs and stone chimneys poked out from under more than 10 feet of water. In the back of their minds, most of the nearly 700 residents probably realized then and there that it was a losing battle. Still, cedar is amazingly rot-resistant and the French were amazingly determined to somehow hang on.

As more floods followed in the 1780s, though, the trickle of land requests outside of the old town site began turning into a flood of its own. It was rapidly becoming clear that the old town was dying.

Ekberg believes the first inhabitants of the new townsite were most likely Jacques Boyer, Jean Baptiste Maurice *dit* Chatillon and Joseph Loisel. He thinks they may have built homes there by 1783. Land grants between the branches of the Gabouri continued to increase as the decade wore on and by the early 1790s even the more affluent citizens were giving up their more substantial homes on the riverbank and building at *les Petites Côtes*.

A 1924 painting by Oscar E. Berninghaus on the wall of the State Capitol in Jefferson City depicts the old townsite of Ste. Genevieve in "le grand champ" and its proximity to the river.

A New Town and a Power Struggle

By the time the move to the new town was being seriously considered, the community was without its leading citizen. Papa Vallé died in 1783, leaving his sons Charles, François II and Jean Baptiste as the richest, most influential young men in town. For a time, though, they were not the dominant force in local government that they are remembered as being. When Henri Peyroux de la Coundreniere succeeded Antonio de Oro as commandant in 1787, he fell into dispute with the Vallé boys almost immediately—as de Oro had also done. The old French title *lieutenant particulier* had been stripped from the position of militia captain when Charles Vallé succeeded his father. A troubled man with alcohol and other personal problems, Charles was not up to carrying the Vallé banner— although he did make a good showing as leader of the Ste. Genevieve militia dispatched to help defend St. Louis from an Anglo-Indian invasion in 1780. When Peyroux came to town, he took over the dual title of commandant and militia captain.

As the old community began to die, both Spain and the Roman Catholic hierarchy seemed strangely reluctant to give permission for the official vestiges of governmental and religious authority to be transferred. Ekberg unearthed numerous letters from officials and priests, imploring that they be removed from the decaying old town, well into the 1790s. Meanwhile, a debate was emerging over where the "new" Ste. Genevieve should be located. A number of inhabitants were already on the higher land between the Gabouri forks. Another settlement was beginning at the mouth of the Saline Creek, south of the village. The salt which was evaporated from the springs there was of vital importance to the

early settlers. It was in the Saline region that Peyroux owned huge tracts of land. During his first years as commandant, Peyroux kept a constant stream of letters routed to his superiors, trying to convince them that the Saline was the ideal place to relocate. He obviously had an ulterior financial motive. As it turned out, when the Saline settlement failed to take root, Peyroux stubbornly refused to move his residence to the new town.

The difficult Peyroux developed a heated rivalry with François Vallé II. When Peyroux left town to try to recruit settlers in 1791 and again in 1792, Vallé was left in charge. Vallé and the town pastor both promptly built houses in the new town and moved without Peyroux's permission. Although Vallé was not yet commandant, his move certainly marked one of the final death knells for the old village. After Peyroux's 1791 trip, Vallé had freed a man in the callaboose, being held for owing a small debt to the commandant. When Vallé refused to pay Peyroux the debt himself, the short-tempered commandant tossed Vallé in the calaboose for five days. These skirmishes with François Vallé II, as much as anything, marked the end for Peyroux. Vallé was appointed civil and military commandant in 1794 and the old town was dead. The church finally received permission to move later in the year. A detailed 1797 map by Nicolas de Finiels identifies the old townsite of Ste. Genevieve as *Ancien village de Ste. Genevieve abandonné*.

The parish priest also had troubles with the difficult Peyroux. Paul von Heiligenstein (known by the French translation, "St. Pierre") was a German Carmelite who had witnessed Washington's victory at Yorktown as a chaplain with the French Expeditionary Force. He was the town's popular pastor in 1785 and 1786 and again from 1789 until he was forced out in 1795. According to Ekberg, Peyroux and the vicar general of American Illinois (another enemy) succeeded in getting rid of the well-liked priest, despite impassioned letters on his behalf from some of the town and region's leading citizens.

A contemporary painting by artist Janet Kraus depicts the new town of Ste. Genevieve as it might have appeared around 1850. The original 4x8 foot watercolor was commissioned and copyrighted by Tim Conley and hangs in the Louisiana Academy which he has recently restored as his place of residence.

A Child's Eye View of Ste. Genevieve

One of the great breaks historians have enjoyed was the arrival in Ste. Genevieve of a nine-year-old boy about 1795. Henry Marie Brackenridge (1786–1871) was the son of a Pittsburgh judge, who wished his son to learn French—the hard way. Brackenridge claimed he knew only two words of French when he arrived to board with the Vital St. Gemme Beauvais family, and that none of the French knew a word of English, except Abbe St. Pierre. Brackenridge quickly adapted to his surroundings though, and grew up to write an autobiography of sorts entitled *Recollections of Persons and Places in the West*. The book gives one of the few intimate portraits of everyday life in colonial Ste. Genevieve—and certainly the only existing look at this world through the eyes of a child. Brackenridge recalled his arrival in the village.

My guardian carried me directly to the house of M. Beauvais, a respectable and comparatively wealthy inhabitant of the village, and he took his departure the same evening. Not a soul in the village except the curate understood a word of English and I was possessed of but two French words—oui and non. I sallied into the street, or rather highway, for the houses were far apart, a large space being occupied for yards and gardens by each. I soon found a crowd of boys at play. Curiosity drew them around me and many questions were put by them, which I answered alternatively with the aid of the aforementioned monosyllables.
"Where have you come from?" — "Oui."
"What is your name?" — "Non."
To the honor of these boys be it spoken, or rather to the honor of their parents who had taught them true politeness, instead of turning me into ridicule as soon as they discovered I was a strange boy, they vied with each other in showing me every act of kindness.

Madame Beauvais insisted on him being baptized. As Brackenridge put it, "She felt some repugnance at putting a little heretic into the same bed with her own children." After the Beauvais family sponsored Brackenridge into the church, he was allowed to address them as father and mother, "and more affectionate, careful, and anxious parents I could not have had." He recalled, in fact, that the couple doted on him to the point of creating "a kind of jealousy" among the other Beauvais children.

Brackenridge's father had wanted him to be fluent in at least two languages. As it turned out, though, as the boy developed skills in French, he lost his ability to speak or understand English. "Who could have supposed that I should be sent home a French boy to learn English?" he quipped. "So completely had every trace disappeared from my memory, with the exception of the words *yes* and *no*, that when sent for occasionally to act as interpreter to some stray Anglo-American, the little English boy, *le petit Anglais*, as they called me, could not comprehend a single word beyond the two monosyllables."

Brackenridge's reflections generally go along with other written opinions on the French inhabitants. A close-knit, fun-loving community, they worked hard in *le grand champ* to get their work out of the way. With the tedious business done, they were free to dance, drink, play cards, ride horses and hunt—which was a combination of necessity and sport.

His sentimental return visit as a young adult in August, 1811 sparked numerous pleasant childhood memories, including being taught how to swim by Jean Baptiste Vallé in the North Gabouri and learning to shoot arrows and speak rudimentary Kickapoo language from Indian children who played with the white youngsters in the village. He looked back with respect on the Beauvais family and the rest of the villagers. The lives and religious practices of the Creole villagers made some visiting European Catholics recoil. No doubt, however, they were sincere and faithful Catholics, who leaned heavily on their faith to survive in the hostile land. Brackenridge fondly remembered kneeling nightly to pray beside Madame Beauvais. "To good seed thus early sown I may ascribe any growth of virtue in a soil that might otherwise have produced only noxious weeds," he recalled.

Le petit Anglais excelled to such an extent in school that he won a miniature set of teacups and saucers as the best reader. He gave those to Catherine, the baby of the Beauvais family, affectionately called "Zouzou." As fate had it, he arrived for his second visit the night before Zouzou, now a young woman, was to be married. Brackenridge kept out of sight all the next day and surprised the family during the wedding celebration. He then knocked on the door and requested Madame Beauvais.

"Madame," said I, "do you recollect the little English boy?" She looked at me a moment and then screamed, "Comment—est il possible? Oui—oui—c'est lui—c'est Henri!" She threw her arms around my neck, while her exclamations brought out the company, grandchildren, cousins, uncles, neighbors, bride and bridegroom; and when the matter was explained, such a bustling frolic took place as was never surpassed even in Ste. Genevieve. The cups and saucers I had presented the bride, and which were the reward of my literary progress, were produced on the table, to show that neither le petit Anglais nor his gift had been forgotten.

American influences had made some major changes in the old town between Brackenridge's first and second visits. Although the landscape was easily recognizable to him, he remarked:

"What changes in the course of ten years, in our short span of life!"

And the French Became Americans

After 38 years under Spanish rule, the Louisiana Territory had briefly lapsed back into French hands in 1800. When Napoleon became desperate to line his war chest, he offered the United States a deal the young nation could not pass up—the entire Louisiana Territory for $15 million. On March 10, 1804, Israel Dodge raised the United States flag over Ste. Genevieve, while Captain Amos Stoddard did the same in St. Louis. Ste. Genevieve's hardy old Frenchmen who would likely have been perfectly contented under a French king were now part of an expanding young republic.

Another key event took place just days before the official American takeover. François Vallé II died at age forty-eight, leaving the Vallé legacy in the hands of younger brother Jean Baptiste. Vallé served the final days of French rule as commandant and then was appointed civil commandant by Stoddard, the territorial governor. He was commandant of the Ste. Genevieve District until Seth Hunt, a U.S. Amy officer, took over. According to local tradition, Vallé continued to serve as town commandant until his death at age eighty-nine in 1849. Noted author Gregory M. Franzwa wrote that the old man continued to dress in colonial-style attire right up till the end, "a living memorial to a dead regime."

General Firmin A. Rozier also recalled the aging Vallé as hearkening back to an earlier time, in his *Rozier's History of the Early Settlement of the Mississippi Valley.*

"But a few years ago one of those patriarchs could be seen in the city of Ste. Genevieve," Rozier wrote in his 1890 history, "leaning on the staff of old age with ease and grace, his head bleached with the snows of nearly a hundred years."

He also recalled a special date from his youth, when the aging commandant and his wife, Jeanne Barbeau Vallé, followed an old French custom and renewed their wedding vows on their fiftieth anniversary in 1833.

Rozier recalled it being a "grand and imposing ceremony to see this venerable couple renewing the first vows of their early affection and love."

Meanwhile Jean Baptiste Vallé's third son, Louis, was appointed by Jefferson to one of the earlier classes at the new U.S. Military Academy at West Point in 1805. He graduated June 13, 1808. Vallé was offered a commission as a second lieutenant in 1808, but turned it down. Instead he returned to Ste. Genevieve and helped advance American ideals at home. Vallé did have one more military duty. In 1815 he was appointed by Territorial Governor William Clark as paymaster for militia in the Missouri Territory. He died tragically in September, 1833 after being bitten by a rabid dog.

A diorama at the Old Courthouse in St. Louis depicts the transfer of the Louisiana Territory.

The Nineteenth Century Arrives

Things were rapidly changing as the new century advanced. More and more Americans crossed the Mississippi, bringing with them new ideas and ways of life—such as the pistol duels in 1811 and 1816 which resulted in the deaths of Dr. Walter Fenwick and Auguste De Mun respectively. The influx of the Americans was reflected in the town's architecture and in its daily life. Gradually Ste. Genevieve became "Americanized."

The Louisiana Academy, conceived in 1807 as the first public school west of the Mississippi, was not only a symbol of the Americanization of the old French Colonial town that began following the Louisiana Purchase; it was also representative of the expansionist and egalitarian foresight of the young United States and its visionary president, Thomas Jefferson.

Nineteenth century Ste. Genevieve had many interesting characters. Famed naturalist John James Audubon arrived, along with Jean Ferdinand Rozier, in 1811, both intent upon making their mark as merchants. Rozier certainly did. A family business bearing the name was in operation as late as 1995 and descen-

dants still operate a store in nearby Perryville. The Rozier family would become one of the wealthiest and most influential in the community during the nineteenth century.

Audubon, however, never seemed to have his heart in it. According to local legend, Rozier would often leave on business trips and return home to find their mercantile establishment closed up and Audubon off, sketching wildlife in the woods. In a short time Audubon left Ste. Genevieve and within a few years had gone on to the work that would make him famous. The naturalist did not leave town with any bitterness toward Rozier, as some have suggested. In fact, the old Louisiana Academy, where the Rozier family lived well into the twentieth century, contained a huge collection of Audubon's stuffed birds, with backgrounds he himself painted. Sadly, only a handful survive today, one being housed at the Ste. Genevieve Museum. Family historian Mary Rozier Sharp, meanwhile, documents several enjoyable visits exchanged between the ex-partners over the remaining years of their lives.

Nineteenth Century Characters

A local actor portrays the famed novelist.

When the *General Pike* steamed up the river in August, 1817, a new era had arrived. Now at least the more affluent citizens could get some of the finer niceties of life. The world was rapidly shrinking.

A young Samuel Clemens also passed through town as a riverboat pilot, storing away amusing anecdotes to draw upon later. Borrowing the pen name "Mark Twain," from a riverboat term, he would later become one of the world's renowned writers. Twain knew the course of the Mississippi like "my hallway at home," he wrote in his *Life on the Mississippi* in which he chronicles his apprenticeship days on the river. In the same book he describes his return to the Midwest later in life to travel once more (this time as a passenger) his beloved river from St. Louis to New Orleans.

We finally got away [from St. Louis] at two in the morning, and when I turned out at six we were rounding to at a rocky point where there was an old stone warehouse—at any rate, the ruins of it; two or three decayed dwelling-houses were near by in the shelter of the leafy hills, but there were no evidences of human or other animal life to be seen. I wondered if I had forgotten the river, for I had no recollection whatever of this place; the shape of the river, too, was unfamiliar; there was nothing in sight anywhere that I could remember having seen before. I was surprised, disappointed, and annoyed.

We put ashore a well-dressed lady and gentleman, and two well-dressed ladylike young girls, together with sundry Russia-leather bags. A strange place for such folk! No carriage was waiting. The party moved off as if they had not expected any, and struck down a winding country road afoot.

But the mystery was explained when we got under way again, for these people were evidently bound for a large town which lay shut in behind a tow-head(i.e., new island) a couple of miles below this landing. I couldn't remember that town; I couldn't place it, couldn't call its name. So I lost part of my temper. I suspected that it might be St. Genevieve—and so it proved to be. Observe what this eccentric river had been about: it had built up this huge, useless towhead directly in front of this town, cut off its river communications, fenced it away completely, and made a "country" town of it. It is a fine old place, too, and deserved a better fate. It was settled by the French, and is a relic of a time when one could travel from the mouths of the Mississippi to Quebec and be on French territory and under French rule all the way.

The change in geography which Twain describes occurred around 1880 when the river shifted its course to the east, away from Ste. Genevieve. The town is still accessible from the river via the Ste. Genevieve Marina and from the Illinois side by car via the Ste. Genevieve-Modoc Ferry and the Chester, Ill.(Mo. Hwy. 51)bridge.—*bn*

The Mississippi Queen docks at Ste. Genevieve's Marina de Gabouri. Located at Mile 121.5, the marina provides convenient access to the town for river travelers.

Another supposed "visitor" was Jesse James. Whether or not it was really the James Gang that robbed the Merchants' Bank of Ste. Genevieve during a daring daylight robbery on May 26, 1873 is still hotly debated by experts. Whoever the daring robbers were, the safe they forced teller Oliver D. Harris to open at gunpoint is now in the Ste. Genevieve Museum. Harris apparently survived the incident without lasting side-effects. He went on to be a key banking leader in the community, publisher of the *Plaindealer* newspaper, and later served as county treasurer.

Famed nineteenth century novelist Ned Buntline was also in town in 1852, albeit not for a very happy visit. He was aboard the ill-fated riverboat *Dr. Franklin II* which exploded north of town and caught fire. It was towed to the dock at Ste. Genevieve. General Firmin A. Rozier wrote that "the sight on board of the steamer was a distressing and mournful one," with the dead piled high and countless others "frightfully mutilated." The dead were buried in a section of the Old Memorial Cemetery.

Rozier himself was a key figure. Forever known as "General" Rozier after he was given the title of general of a local militia regiment that never took up arms, the banker/attorney was one of the town's wealthiest and most influential citizens. The general served as both a state representative and a state senator. Said to be acquaintances of such notables as Henry Clay, John C. Calhoun,

John J. Crittenden and Thomas Hart Benton, he made one final attempt at establishing a school in the decrepit Louisiana Academy building in the 1850s. Using his own immense funds, he launched the Ste. Genevieve Academy in 1849 and added a brick wing to the old stone building in 1854. His school thrived until the Civil War took the faculty and many of his students. He was influential in the construction of the Plank Road (connecting Ste. Genevieve to Farmington and the lead country of St. Francois County) and fought tirelessly for a railroad line—something he missed seeing by two years. Later in his life, the general became deeply interested in the old town's history and was its first true historian. He wrote the first history of the town, *Rozier's History of the Early Settlement of the Mississippi*.

Ste. Genevieve produced several politicians of state-wide significance. John Scott, Missouri's first representative in the U.S. House and the father of Missouri's public school system, lived the final fifty-six years of his life in the town. The controversial Scott, renowned for wearing his pistols in plain view while arguing cases in court—and for supposedly using them to intimidate judges and jurors—had served two terms as a territorial delegate to Congress when Missouri became a state. He was elected as Missouri's first congressman, serving until his support for John Quincy Adams cost him popular support back home—where Andrew Jackson was wildly popular. Scott, one of the forty-one men who framed Missouri's state constitution, died in his home in Ste. Genevieve in 1861. He is buried in the Memorial Cemetery.

The Merchants Bank once stood on the southwest corner of Main and Merchant Streets. Some say it was Jesse James that robbed the bank in 1873. Later known as the Rottler Building, it was razed in 1934 to allow for the construction of the Standard Oil Gas Station. That building still stands at that corner and serves today as an annex to the Ste. Genevieve Fire Department.

Another key figure was Dr. Lewis F. Linn, immortalized as "Missouri's Model Senator." Linn was most noted as a leading voice for acquiring the Oregon Territory. He and Missouri's senior senator, the renowned Thomas Hart Benton, formed a potent one-two punch in the Oregon debate during the 1830s and 1840s. Linn introduced a bill on February 7, 1838 to obtain the territory. It failed by a tiny majority. The vision of Linn and Benton was realized a decade later, but the good doctor did not live to see it. A practicing physician, he returned to Ste. Genevieve in 1843 to help fight a cholera epidemic and died of an aneurysm. Linn cut his political teeth in Ste. Genevieve, serving as a county commissioner (or judge), then a state senator, before entering the national arena.

Lewis F. Linn

General Rozier helped deify Linn, claiming that Linn once corrected Henry Clay on the Senate floor, after which Clay bowed and replied "It is sufficient that it come from the Senator from Missouri." On another occasion, according to Rozier, James Buchanan (then *president pro tem* of the Senate) halted Linn before he could present a roll of bills. "Doctor, we will save you trouble," Buchanan supposedly exclaimed. "If you recommend them, we will pass the whole bundle."

While Rozier's depiction of Linn's Washington esteem seems questionable, he was certainly a noted early U.S. senator and is certainly a familiar name to any students of the Oregon Territory or the Oregon Trail. His house still stands on Merchant Street, as does the cut stone Dufour building which he purchased as an office in 1831.

When Lewis Linn's body was exhumed from the Crestlawn Cemetery to be relocated to the Memorial Cemetery in the 1940s, gravediggers were surprised to find that the good senator's corpse, his face visible through a glass window in the coffin, had been perfectly mummified.
—Photo courtesy, Basler Funeral Home

Had he possessed good health, it is very likely that General Rozier's younger brother, Charles C. "Major" Rozier (1830-1897), might have become as renowned on a state level as any of the aforementioned statesmen. Considered one of the finest probate lawyers in the state, the sometimes-newspaper publisher was certainly among the sharpest nineteenth-century Ste. Genevievans. An invalid since early childhood, the major walked with a pair of canes. Rozier was one of the original members of the board of regents of the Southeast Missouri Normal School (now Southeast Missouri State University) and helped select Cape Girardeau as the school's site in 1873. He had to give up this and other prestigious positions due to the agony that travel caused him. His physical condition likely doomed him in losing campaigns for state auditor in 1864 and 1868, as well. He was also one of the city's earliest newspaper publishers, printing *The Creole* and later *The Plaindealer*. The highly-esteemed Major Rozier served two terms as mayor of Ste. Genevieve (1874-1877 and 1879-1897), dying in office some two weeks before the death of his brother Firmin.

STE. GENEVIEVE PLAINDEALER.

$1.50 IN ADVANCE.

NO. 28

"LIBERTY AND UNION—NOW AND FOREVER—ONE AND INSEPERABLE."—WEBSTER.

STE. GENEVEIVE, MO., FRIDAY, AUGUST 31, 1860.

Ste. Genevieve's Memorial Cemetery is the resting place of the town's early pioneers. It remains a peaceful retreat in the center of town.

❧ A Celebration and a New Century ❧

In 1885 the city celebrated the centennial of the move from the old townsite to the new. Almost canceled due to a national depression and bank failure, the celebration was doomed by horrid weather and some questionable organization. According to reports, it was already unbearably hot by 9A.M. A couple of the key scheduled speakers were nowhere to be found when their turns came to talk. The aging General Rozier was among the speakers, reading a long text that would later make up the bulk of his book. Unfortunately, his voice did not carry well and the restless crowd, unable to hear and squiriming in the blistering heat, had to be quieted twice by Mayor Charles Rozier, the general's brother.

A torrential rainstorm ended a miserably hot ordeal for spectators, but left the town a muddy mess. "A few minutes of the storm was sufficient to change from one of life and gaiety to a wild waste of slush and mud," wrote *Ste. Genevieve Herald* publisher Joseph A. Ernst. The storm also caused the roof of the skating rink to collapse, although no one was injured. The chaos inspired Ernst to suggest that since organizers claimed they hadn't had proper time to prepare, perhaps planning should begin at once for the "next Centennial" in 1985! It must be noted, though, that Ernst was more often than not locked in a duel of the pens with *Ste. Genevieve Fair Play*— especially when it was published by Henry S. Shaw. Shaw was a member of the local school board, for whom Ernst worked as a teacher and school principal. Shaw, meanwhile, was on the steering committee of the centennial celebration, whose leadership Ernst belittled in the *Herald* for months. He also pointed out that former Secretary of the Interior Carl Schurz had been partying hearty. "If the rain hadn't set in," Ernst quipped, "he would have created a beer famine."

Shaw, naturally, painted a more positive picture of the celebration he helped plan, putting most of the blame for problems on the operators of the riverboat *Will S. Hays.* "It would have been a splendid and enjoyable affair if the weather had been cooler and the beer seller on the *Hays* a little more decent," he wrote. "It was good enough anyway."

Both papers skewered the *Hays* and its beer vendors. "The commander ... and the crowd of toughs and thieves to whom he sold his bar

A turn-of-the-century gala event at the old Armory Hall in Ste. Genevieve captured by photographer Vincent J. Dunker

and restaurant privileges acted in a shameful manner," The *Fair Play* reported. According to Shaw, the ship was intentionally held back, keeping the captive audience as long as possible. Not only was no free water available, but purportedly a barrel of ice water, brought by a customer, was thrown overboard. After fleecing his passengers, the vendor who was operating without a license, had the nerve to set up a stand just outside the city limits, competing with local vendors. He was soon sent on his way.

The 1890s saw considerable change in the old town. Odile Vallé, widow of leading merchant Felix Vallé and an important figure in her own right, died in 1894. The year 1897 saw Ste. Genevieve lose General Rozier, Mayor Charles Rozier, Emilie "Mammy" Shaw and business leaders Emile Vogt and Nicolas Wehner. It also saw probably the worst windstorm in the town's history strike on June 19, 1897, flattening several barns and blowing roofs off a number of houses.

All Aboard!
The Railroad Comes to Town

The town eagerly awaited the arrival of the railroad during the late 1890s, anticipating a tremendous increase in the local business activity. John Tlapek of St. Mary spearheaded the local line, with the backing of Missouri railroad magnate and historian, Louis Houck. Although there was considerable debate in Ste. Genevieve, most community leaders seemed to be firmly behind the idea. As the author of a letter to the editor in the December 11, 1897 *Herald* put it, "Without a [rail]road,

Ste. Genevieve must pass into history, a relic of the past." Well it might have. The arrival certainly helped, as did the coming of electricity and the 1900 arrival of telephone service. The town never grew rapidly, though, turning down options of having Southeast Missouri State University and Pittsburgh Plate Glass come to town.

The first train arrives in Ste. Genevieve on June 11, 1899.

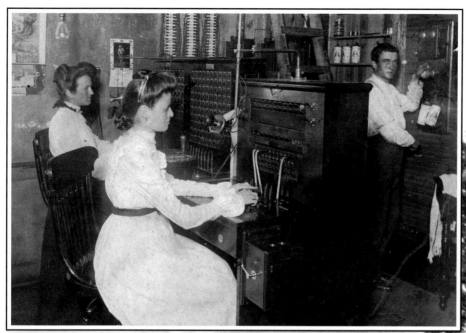

Odile Janis and Catherine Lelie operate the switchboards in Ste. Genevieve's telephone office which was located in the Dufour Stone Building(now Tlapek Real Estate). Wire Chief LeClere Janis looks on.

The Landing Called Little Rock

One negative that came with the railroad was the virtual death of the Little Rock port. Henry Wilder had laid out platts and made serious plans to incorporate a town called Little Rock, (named for a rock that stood out of the river some fifteen to twenty feet before being blasted by the U.S. Army Corps of Engineers) north of town on Little Rock Road. Chief among the many landing buildings was his own impressive late eighteenth century mansion, possibly built by Michael Placet and later owned by Jean Baptiste Vallé (both senior and junior). The railroad ended all plans of a Little Rock community and the grand house burned to the ground on February 20, 1936. The foundation of the house is about all that remains today of Little Rock, other than a railroad crossing, the ferry landing and a barge loading facility operated by Mississippi Lime.

The Ste. Genevieve-Modoc Ferry, appropriately named *The French Connection*, operates daily connecting the two banks of the old French corridor. Motorists and bicyclers can easily cross the river to visit the historically significant sites of Prairie du Rocher, Fort de Chartres, Fort Kaskaskia and the Pierre Menard Home.

ABOVE: A railroad dedication ceremony at Little Rock Landing. People in the photo are unidentified except for a young Rev. C.L. van Tourenhout(center) wearing a collar and white hat. BELOW: Little Rock had been the boat landing for steamboats during the 1800s. The old stone warehouse, water tower and Henry Wilder's residence against the bluff are pictured in this Vince Dunker photo.

Little Rock Remembered...
Ste. Genevieve Transfer Ferry

Until 1961 there was still some activity at Little Rock Landing. It was in that year that the Ste. Genevieve to Kellogg(also known as the Thomure-Kellogg) railroad ferry ceased operation in favor of "longbarrel" trains to move great numbers of freight cars using railroad bridges to cross the wide river.

Little Rock Landing was a common destination for a Sunday afternoon family drive. There, visitors would watch as dark plumes of smoke billowed from a locomotive engine as she backed freight cars down the incline, then up the cradle to the bow of the sidewheeler. Finally, the cars were eased onto one of the three parallel tracks on the ferry. Each track could hold six cars.

Once loaded, the boat backed away from the pilings and made its slow journey to the Illinois side, docking at Kellogg.

The original wooden-hulled "Ste. Genevieve" was placed into service in 1904. It was damaged in 1912 when the Mississippi was choked solid with ice flows. It was repaired however, and operated another six years until it sank, while loaded, at Kellogg in 1918.

The Missouri-Illinois Railroad purchased the operation in 1921 from Illinois Southern and readied the second "Ste. Genevieve."

With her six boilers and twenty-eight foot paddlewheels, she worked the crossing from 1922 until June, 1961. Remnants of the incline are still visible when the river is low. –bn

A 1948 photograph of the Ste. Genevieve
Transfer Ferry by Missouri State Photographer
Gerald Massie

Little Rock
Remembered…

ABOVE: An HO scale model of the Ste. Genevieve-Kellogg sidewheel steamer and railroad incline by Ste. Genevieve modeler Lewis Pruneau is housed in the Ste. Genevieve Museum.

The early Ste. Genevieve was damaged in 1912 when the Mississippi became choked by ice. It was repaired and continued to operate until it sank, while loaded, at Kellogg in 1918.

In Quest of the Stone...

When it comes to establishing an earlier founding date for Ste. Genevieve, one story stands above the rest—if not for its documentation, then at least for its intrigue.

While hunting during the fall of 1881, Leon Jokerst, a leading Ste. Genevieve businessman and Union Civil War veteran, who would later serve as sheriff (1885-1889), as well as county treasurer and city alderman, was said to have found an old well on the eroding riverbank where the old town site had been. The exposed stone well was sticking up "like a chimney or tower," out of the disappearing bank. It would soon be swallowed up by the river. Jokerst supposedly found a stone with the year "1732" clearly carved in it and chiseled part of it off. The only known report of this major find is a letter from Captain Gustavus St. Gem, another leading local citizen and Union Civil War veteran. St. Gem had served as collector for the Port of St. Louis, under President Rutherford B. Hayes and had apparently just returned to Ste. Genevieve by this time. Either a portion or all of a short letter from Captain St. Gem to Goodspeed Publishing appears in the company's "History of Southeast Missouri," which was printed in 1888–the first known written history of the region. In it, St. Gem described Jokerst's discovery in some detail, lamenting that he didn't save the entire stone, which "certainly would have been appreciated as a valuable relic." He also noted (just six or so years after its discovery) that Jokerst still possessed the rock, "with a written memorandum attached thereto," and would pull it out to show interested parties from time to time.

Verifying this event has thus far proven futile. Jokerst died suddenly in 1909 and all seven of his children had already left Ste. Genevieve. If the rock did exist, the chances of it still surviving and being located are extremely slim. Both Louis Houck and Father Francis Yealy mention the story in their later histories. Yealy's footnote refers to Houck, however, and Houck's to Goodspeed. It appears that St. Gem's letter is the only original account. Interestingly, General Firmin A. Rozier did not mention the find in his own history, published just two years after the Goodspeed book. Rozier was a contemporary of both Jokerst and St. Gem, serving with both on the committees that planned the town's 1885 centennial celebration of the move from the old townsite.

Appreciation For Town's History Grows

Exactly when the outside world—or local residents for that matter—began to truly appreciate Ste. Genevieve's remarkable history is hard to determine. General Rozier began to do research possibly as early as the 1870s. In 1888 Goodspeed Publishing in Chicago published *History of Southeast Missouri,* looking at each community in the region. Rozier was among the contributors on the Ste. Genevieve section, along with Captain Gustavus St. Gem, whose account of Leon Jokerst's 1881 discovery of a stone with the date "1732" carved in it has been one source of documention of the town's earlier founding date (*See story, facing page*). St. Gem was frequently quoted in the Missouri Historical Society's publications of the day, as was his older sister, Augustine (Mrs. Louis C.) Menard, the great-grand daughter of Vital St. Gemme Beauvais and the daughter-in-law of the renowned Pierre Menard.

"Mrs. Menard is a woman of wonderful memory, and is perhaps the best posted person, regarding the history of this country, of anyone now living," the Goodspeed book noted.

Ida M. Schaaf of nearby St. Mary also became a preeminent area historian as the early 1900s wore on. Another key contribution was made by State Normal School (now Southeast Missouri State) Professor Robert S. Douglass who wrote his own *History of Southeast Missouri* in 1912.

The arrival of Charles Peterson, a bright young landscape architect, turned architectural historian, was a crucial moment in the city's history. Peterson founded the National Park Service's Historic American Buildings Survey, which recorded and catalogued the city's historic structures. It also gave 1,000 unemployed architects jobs during the height of the Depression. He also authored a 1941 pamphlet, "A Guide to Ste. Genevieve, With Notes on its Architecture," and helped beat the drum for the appreciation and preservation of Ste. Genevieve's historic architecture.

It was probably the 1935 bicentennial celebration, though, that opened the most eyes to Ste. Genevieve's heritage. The Bicentennial celebration also saw Father Francis J. Yealy's book, *Sainte Genevieve, The Story of Missouri's Oldest Settlement,* published by the bicentennial committee.

A nineteenth century view of a dirt-lined Merchant Street taken near the corner of Third Street looking east shows a number of Ste. Genevieve's earlier structures. From the left is the Roy House and the two-story Arlington Hotel which sat on the lots presently occupied by the Orris Theatre, the Ste. Genevieve Winery and the Craft Depot. Next are the Senator Linn House(today's Wipfler Home) and the Dufour Stone Building (now Tlapek Real Estate) which Linn used as an office. Both buildings still stand today. Crossing Second Street we see the Jesse Robbins House(the restored home of Bill Bader). Further down the street a group of three people visit in front of the Lewis Bogy House(not visible) while two horses draw a wagon up the street.
—Photo courtesy of Lucille Basler

A Tale of Two Photographers

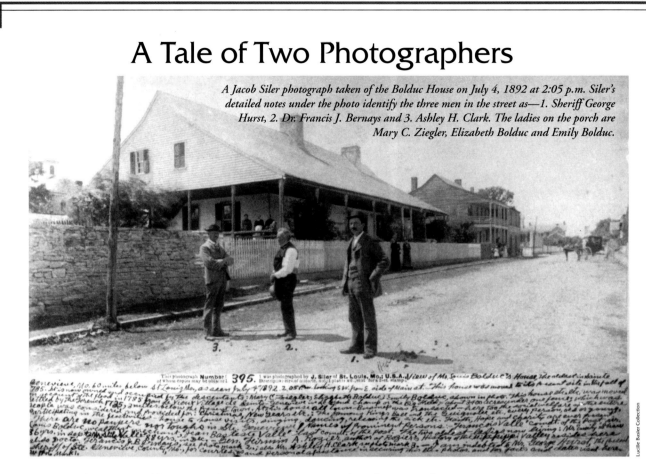

A Jacob Siler photograph taken of the Bolduc House on July 4, 1892 at 2:05 p.m. Siler's detailed notes under the photo identify the three men in the street as—1. Sheriff George Hurst, 2. Dr. Francis J. Bernays and 3. Ashley H. Clark. The ladies on the porch are Mary C. Ziegler, Elizabeth Bolduc and Emily Bolduc.

Another type of historian began to emerge as the photographic process was being perfected. Two turn-of-the-century photographers left images that give impressions of a Ste. Genevieve in the late 1800s and early 1900s. Jacob Siler was a turn-of-the-century St. Louis druggist-turned-photographer who had a remarkable appreciation for the camera as an instrument of documentation. He had a particular interest in historic architecture and made some detailed exposures of the remaining French Creole architecture in the old Illinois Country.

Siler had the endearing habit of jotting down detailed notes on the bottom or backs of his prints. He normally listed the date, time of day, place he was standing and direction he was facing. He often jotted down historic information about the building or individuals he was shooting. In his book, Siler's Historic Photos, apparently printed for the St. Louis World's Fair in 1904, he noted that "the views are selected to delineate some historic event or point" and "the author's sole aim is to present the largest number of facts and figures in the least space and lowest possible price."

Duane Sneddeker, photo archivist for the Missouri Historical Society, noted that Siler often shot Civil War battlefields and other historic sites and that as an elderly man, he was said to regale young acquaintances with stories that he had been a Union spy during the Civil War. Many questions remain unanswered about the elusive Siler. *—mle*

If Siler was St. Louis' druggist-turned-photographer, then Vincent J. Dunker was Ste. Genevieve's photographer-turned-inventor. Dunker was a portrait photographer whose efforts to find a more efficient way to photograph school children led to his perfecting a 35 millimeter long-roll camera in 1924. A St. Louis photographer, hearing of the product, prevailed upon Dunker and purchased the camera for one hundred dollars. The inventor's second fabrication found a similar purchaser. At that point, Dunker abandoned the idea of taking school pictures and instead concentrated his efforts on the design and manufacture of long-roll cameras. In

1925 he patented a hand printer which used 250-foot rolls of photographic paper. He also patented a direct-to-print camera booth for use at fairs and carnivals. These units were shipped as far away as Hong Kong and one was used locally at the 1935 Bicentennial in Ste. Genevieve.

In 1955, Dunker sold his portrait business along with most of his negatives to his apprentice, Betty Schwent Donze. It is to her credit that most of Dunker's early 1900 images of the streets and families of Ste. Genevieve have been preserved these many years. Some of his images grace the pages of this book. —*bn*

A man crosses the street at the corner of Third and Merchant in this Dunker photograph. Behind him are seen today's Anvil restaurant, Boverie's General Merchandise(white building), and the Old Brick House(also painted white). Further down the street, a horse-drawn bus awaits lodgers at Vorst's Southern Hotel to be transported to their steamboat at Little Rock landing. The Hettig-Nauman house sits on the Seraphin Street hill in the distance. The corner of the Okenfuss Hardware Building can just be seen behind the trees of the Courthouse Square. At the right of the photo, is the Jokerst-Yealy Building.

The
World Comes To Ste. Genevieve

One of the big moments in Ste. Genevieve history took place in 1935. For four days that summer, the world came to Ste. Genevieve in a bicentennial bash that was staggering in its dimensions. Despite the Great Depression, the town planned four years or more in advance for the four-day epic to be held August 19-22. President Franklin D. Roosevelt and First Lady Eleanor Roosevelt were both invited, but neither were able to attend. FDR, though, did open the festivities August 19 by speaking to the huge crowd over a speakerphone. (The special phone line cost $400 to be installed.) Governor Guy Park and first-term U.S. Senator Harry S. Truman were among the notables who did attend in person. Mayor Harry J. Petrequin made an elegant speech. He noted that the combination of French, Spanish and American heritage had given Ste. Genevieve "a certain quaint atmosphere which can scarcely be found in any other section of our land."

"We invite you to turn away from the monotony of the every day and to make this visit, in the nature of a pilgrimage to a shrine of history," Petrequin said, in possibly the first exercise in promoting heritage tourism in Ste. Genevieve. The mayor proved to be a golden wordsmith as he neared his climax.

"See the portrayal of the beautiful history of our pioneer forefathers as a rich, old tapestry, with all its glory and color, scenes woven in the cloth of time," he intoned, "made bit by bit during the slow passage of two centuries, made up of all the clean, bright colors of their simple joys, shot through with the golden light of their homestead hearth."

A whopping 1,200-person cast was assembled for the epic pageant, which was told in song, drama and poetry. The July 27, 1935, *Fair Play* urged parents to make sure their children attended pageant practice regularly. "A flop would make our town the brunt of a nation-wide joke," the paper extolled. Everyone pulled together and no such calamity occurred.

Written and directed by Perryville priest Rev. J. B. Platisha, the play and the giant stage were considered huge successes. Valle Spring was dammed to create a small lake and a 14,240-seat arena was put together, along with a triangular "island" in the lake, with a miniature model of the old village. During the pageant, it was inundated with water, to depict the flood of 1785.

A special train ran on the Frisco line from St. Louis each evening and people poured in. The brand-new museum had more than 2,000 visitors each day, while more than 3,000 patrons paid each evening of the pageant. The bicentennial came out in the black by more than $2,000, but more importantly, opened the eyes of many around the nation to the quaint little French town nestled in the Missouri hills. People began to see that Mayor Petrequin was right. Ste. Genevieve was an ideal destination for an historical pilgrimage.

A Black Night in History

Other events of the decade were not quite so festive as the bicentennial celebration. America had just begun experiencing hard times when the autumn of 1930 saw the summer heat subside and trees throughout Missouri's oldest town start to change colors. In Ste. Genevieve, a fairly large transient black population had established itself, living in shacks north of town and in other locations, such as the east end of Merchant Street. Most of these transients worked in the lime kilns and stone quarries. When two white Ste. Genevieve men went out to blow off some steam on the night of October 11, a disturbing chapter in the old town's history was about to be written.

Harry Panchot, 40, and Paul Leo Ritter, 38, decided shortly after midnight to visit a black dance at a shack on Merchant, according to the October 18, 1930 Ste. Genevieve Herald. While there, two black men, Columbus Jennings and Lee Taylor, accompanied by a black woman named Vera Rogers, asked them to drive them to Little Rock Landing for a craps game. Ritter later testified that the trio paid the white men $1.50 for the ride.

When they arrived at the Frisco Railroad trestle, near the landing, the passengers produced guns. According to Ritter's testimony, they took $10, a watch and a fountain pen from him and $35 from Panchot. Taylor then shot Panchot through the heart and a shuffle ensued between Ritter and Taylor. Rogers supposedly encouraged Taylor to shoot him, which he did. Panchot, who was dead, and Ritter, now paralyzed, were dragged to the edge of the river and dumped in.

"I was paralyzed from the waist down, and could not use my feet but I managed to keep afloat by paddling with my hands," Ritter reported before dying after an unsuccessful operation to remove the bullet from his spine. "The woman noticed it and began throwing large stones at me. One of them hit me in the head." Guards on a confiscated liquor barge nearby heard the shots and pulled him out of the river.

By late morning the town was in an uproar, as news of the attempted double-murder spread. "Never before within the recollection of any man or woman living here, was Ste. Genevieve stirred to the pitch that she was last Sunday," began the Herald's lead.

The three culprits were rounded up Sunday and all three confessed, although their depositions did not entirely agree and were "honeycombed with statements intended to lessen the bitter feeling that they knew existed against them," in the Herald's words.

Other communities of the period resorted to lynchings. Fortunately, Ste. Genevieve avoided such a stigma, although rumors exist that lynchings did occur at other points in the town's history. To avoid any possible trouble, the prisoners were taken to Hillsboro immediately after interrogation and then on to St. Louis.

It was then that an act that many would rather forget was carried out.

"A large number of men in automobiles visited various quarters of town and outlying districts, warning the Negro population to move away from this vicinity" the Herald reported. "And that warning was heeded as evidenced by the fact that all day Monday they could be seen going out afoot, by auto and on trains. By Monday night practically all of the Negroes who had been imported from the South to work at the lime kilns and in the different stone quarries had disappeared."

Unfortunately, the itinerant blacks were not the only ones scared off.

"Quite a number of our local Negro citizens who, let it be said to their credit, refused to mingle with those brought in here, also departed to remain away until the trouble subsided," Fred A. Ernst wrote in the Herald. "Others remained in their homes and attended peacefully to their own business. They were not molested."

"This ruling affected about 200 Negroes and Monday morning the exodus began," Fair Play editor LeClere Janis reported. "The banished Negroes left by car, train and some walked out of town. By 5 p.m. that evening only two (black) families remained in Ste. Genevieve."

Pleas from Sheriff Louis Ziegler and the Commission for Inter-Racial Cooperation in Atlanta to the governor, led to the arrival of about 80 members of Companies M and H, 40th Infantry of the Missouri National Guard. According to the Herald, the Guard found the town "very quiet and orderly." Late Tuesday afternoon the Guard left; the situation appeared under control.

Sadly, one handful of men had different ideas. The Ribault (usually spelled "Ribeau" during the early 20th century) family had been a respected mulatto family for nearly 100 years. Since 1837, the family had peacefully occupied the historic Bequette-Ribault House on St. Mary Road.

Leola Amoureux Duckett fondly remembered childhood visits with the Ribault family while staying with her uncle, Boyington Amoureux.

"The self-taught Ribault men were well informed, their store of knowledge was incredible and they loved to talk on many subjects," she said in her family biography, *The Amoureux Family in Ste. Genevieve.* "It was enjoyable, educational and sometimes amusing to listen to them."

That night "a mob of self-appointed vigilantes," in Janis' words, drove to the historic house, then occupied by Long, Levi and Louis "Cap" Ribault. According to Ernst, the group "arrived with guns, daggers, etc." They demanded that Louis Ribault, a postal carrier, come outside. According to the Fair Play, the mob members assured the other Ribault brothers "that no harm would come of the visit and that Louis would be escorted out of town without bodily harm."

As fate would have it, while the men were standing in the road, "discussing among themselves what to do," a passing motorist ran over one of the mob members. In the darkness and excitement, Louis Ribault slipped away to safety. According to the Herald, the popular Ribault caught a train for St. Louis, where he checked into a sanitarium.

To Sheriff Ziegler's credit, he soon had six of the men in jail and put out another call for the National Guard. According to the Fair Play, "machine guns were stationed in front of the jail and the town was patrolled during the remainder of the night."

Brothers Felix and LeClere Janis set type for the weekly edition in the press room of the Ste. Genevieve Fair Play.

The beloved Reverend C.L. vanTourenhout, pastor of the Ste. Genevieve Catholic Church, made a plea Wednesday, before a gathering of some 250 business men, for "the restoration of peace and good will."

"Standing in a hall packed with citizens, while about him were the officers of two National Guard companies, the white-haired father, who for 47 years has administered to the spiritual ills of this parish, called for the complete cooperation of every citizen in combating racial disorders and mob violence," the Fair Play reported.

"Ste. Genevieve has always boasted openly of its good name and of its law-abiding citizens," vanTourenhout said. "If this is true, it is now their duty to curb, in every way possible, this spirit of racial animosity that has been expressing itself during the last few days."

The longtime priest showed his mettle during the emergency, not only speaking calming words, but reportedly hiding out the highly-respected Bazile family, long-time church attendants, during the chaos.

The National Guard left again, leaving the Buchholtz-Kiefer Post of the American Legion in charge of security. Things were getting back to normal, although the outside world apparently was abuzz with rumors of total anarchy in Ste. Genevieve.

"Many long distance telephone calls were made—and it is surprising how much information had been rumored about," the Herald reported. "Inquiries were made to find out whether there was rioting and bloodshed on the streets among our citizens and whether it were true that a fire had started here that got beyond the control of the department, besides dozens of other ridiculous and preposterous questions."

Both local newspapers blamed the St. Louis daily papers for spreading unsubstantiated rumors about riots taking place here. Ernst alleged that the papers "drew on their prolific imaginations to paint as black and revolting a picture as possible. Their purpose no doubt was to sell extra copes of their newspapers." He later called them "lowbrow scandal-mongers."

Cap Ribault later returned, but most of the native blacks did not. According to the Fair Play, they (but not others) would have been welcomed back.

"The Legionnaires adopted a resolution guaranteeing a protection to certain native property-owning blacks whenever they might wish to return to their homes, though it was definitely stated that no other Negroes would be permitted to return to this community."

The black population in Ste. Genevieve never reached its former numbers again, although a significant number were said to be here during the 1950s and 1960s–with many living in shacks high atop a bluff, north of town until they burned.

In an interview in the early 1990s, Jack Brooks, son of the highly-respected Will Brooks, said that he learned more about prejudice in four years in the armed forces than he had in 18 years in Ste. Genevieve. He also noted that a cruel sign at a football game at Flat River the year he integrated the Ste. Genevieve school system, was the only blatant prejudice he faced growing up. He also noted that there were certain blacks who did not fit community guidelines for acceptable behavior and that the blacks wishing to be accepted, avoided them.

While not remaining true to its color-blind colonial tradition, Ste. Genevieve seemed to be reasonably tolerant over the years. With the ugly incident at the Bequette-Ribault House standing as the only known exception, the town seemed able and willing to discriminate between upstanding, respectable black families and blacks who were not such good citizens.

Generally speaking, if a black family in Ste. Genevieve met the behavioral standards of the best of the local white citizenry, its presence could be tolerated. While not a glowing testimony to the town, neither has its history of race relations cast the historic city in a particularly negative light, comparatively speaking.

Missouri's Last Hanging

In 1937, the last execution by hanging in the State of Missouri was conducted in Ste. Genevieve. The location was on the grounds of the County Poor Farm on Little Rock Road. Hurt Hardy, Jr. was hung from the gallows on February 26 for the brutal murder of Ethel Fahnestock who had spurned his romantic advances.

Reports in the St. Louis newspapers indicated that some 400 people were crowded around the gallows with another 1000 including women and children trying to peer through the 16-foot stockade fence. Insinuating that locals turned this into a gala event, "even bringing their children," one St. Louis newspaper gloated, "Ste. Genevieve—Missouri's oldest community and heir to centuries of French culture—has proved as primitive as the rest of us when humanity is allowed to be exposed to the raw."

In response, druggist Mildred Rutledge, whose drugstore was located directly across from the jail where the crowds first assembled, wrote, "This morbidly curious crowd you refer to so scathingly was not composed of our citizens, but of people from all over the state."

Another Ste. Genevieve citizen was appalled at the insinuations of the out-of-town newspapers and wrote, "Yes, the hanging which took place in Missouri's oldest community was a spectacle, and we citizens, who try to carry on the French culture of centuries to which we have fallen heir, bitterly resent the spectacle which outside people made of the hanging of Hurt Hardy. If the number of people counted in the photographs you spoke of were from Ste. Genevieve, we would bow our heads in shame. The effect of all this ugly publicity is to cast a shadow of shame over Ste. Genevieve and to leave the impression that the inhabitants of this city are people of a low nature, bloodthirsty and mentally depraved, in spite of their being heirs to centuries of culture and other elevating influences."

Such was Ste. Genevieve's sense of pride in its citizenry and heritage. The inhumane nature of execution by hanging led to the eventual outlawing of the practice in favor of lethal gas.

The County Poor Farm on North Main Street was built in 1912 for destitute people who would work the farm in return for room and board. In 1937, it was the site of the last hanging in the State of Missouri. It later served as a county nursing home and was then abandoned for nearly twenty years. The building was renovated in 1995 by Dick and Suzanne Greminger.

One structure in downtown Ste. Genevieve has a bit of history that bridges 50 years between the 1935 Bicentennial and the 250th celebration in 1985.

Shortly after the ashes of the old Missouri Theatre on Main Street cooled, the owner, Martin Operle, had a new theatre built on Merchant Street in 1932. It was named the Orris Theatre after the Orris flour which was milled in St. Mary. It was grand in its day and even boasted one of the first air-conditioning systems utilizing well water on the property. Two years later, a restaurant was added onto the east side of the Orris expressly to serve the crowds that were anticipated for the Bicentennial. That addition would later be known to locals as "Cap" Donze's Cut-Rate and bus stop, followed by Big Ts Longhouse, and a pizza parlor.

The Orris continued to be used as a movie theatre until 1975, having completely lost the grandeur known to all residents who grew up on the movies in its heyday. The newly formed Ste. Genevieve Council of Performing Arts rented the building in 1976 and produced a wide variety of plays from *You're a Good Man Charlie Brown* to *The Effects of Gamma Rays on Man-in-the-Moon Marigolds*. The most popular of the plays using all local talent was *Ten Nights in a Bar Room* which starred the beloved Dr. Reed Marts and former Valle football coach Ralph Thomure. The Knights of Columbus sang the Whiffenpoof Song between acts. It was standing room only every night in the 300 seat theatre. Whether it was the popularity of the "star-studded" cast or a misunderstood banner

BACKGROUND PHOTO: The neon marquis and color photo of the cast and crew of "Ten Nights in a Bar Room"(1980) are superimposed upon the 1932 photo of the Orris Theatre.

hanging conspicuously across Merchant Street proclaiming "ten nights in a bar room" perhaps unintentionally leading some theatre goers to expect free drinks on the house, it was, nonetheless, the biggest financial success in the theatre group's history. But, relying entirely on volunteer energy, by the mid-1980s the Council of Performing Arts was dissolved. In a small way, theatre was taken up by the Steigerhaus Players under the direction of Rob and Layla Beckerman, who continued to do mysteries out of their bed and breakfast business.

In 1983, four ambitious young men in their twenties purchased the run down Orris Theatre. Mark and Dan Monia, Bob Roth and Dick Greminger completely gutted the place, leveled the floor and created Creole porch façades in keeping with the French character of the town. It was opened as a bar which fea-

tured rock and country bands. Coincidentally, it opened in 1985 in time for the 250th celebration, the stage area used to host academic lectures, the winning submitted play *A Celebration of Time*, *Quilters*, and *Flying High*, a musical about the Audubon and Rozier partnership complete with feathered bird costumes.

Although rock and roll and country bands are the mainstay, they've opened their stage for various cultural events including the *Les Amis' La Fête Française* lectures, plays, and quartets. Interestingly and in typical Ste. Genevieve style, beneath the rolling stage are horseshoe pits, a popular Ste. Genevieve pastime.

It is now owned by Dick and Susanne Greminger who also bought and restored (along with Bill Lurk) the adjoining restaurant building which is appropriately named Sirro's —that's Orris spelled backwards. —*psn*

The Bolduc House(in foreground) and the LeMeilleur House (once known as the Convent of the Sisters of Loretto and Detchemendy Hotel) prior to their 1950s restoration.

The Bolduc and the Rise of Tourism

In 1949 the sagging Bolduc House was purchased by Mary Reber, who donated it to the Colonial Dames of America in the State of Missouri. It was painstakingly restored under the direction of the renowned architect, Ernest Allen Connally. The house opened its doors as a tourist site and museum in May, 1958. Many people see that date as the official beginning of Ste. Genevieve being a tourist destination.

Buildings do not regenerate and the town would be full of deteriorating houses, or minus the historic structures altogether, had concerned individuals not arisen during the 1940s, '50s and '60s. From its opening in 1912, Mississippi Lime Company has been extremely generous in giving back to the community. The Bolduc restoration, as well as the saving of the Bolduc-LeMeilleur House and the Linden House, came about largely because of the generosity of Harry and Constance Mathews. Harry Mathews, Jr. was president of Mississippi Lime during this period and Mrs. Mathews was a leader in the Colonial Dames. Both organizations have played major parts in the preservation of the town's heritage. Mrs. Mathews' concern for the community's historic fabric has been carried on by her daughter, Margaret M. Jenks.

CENTER PHOTO: Ribbon cutting ceremony in the doorway of the newly restored Bolduc House. National President of the Colonial Dames Society(left) is joined by Ernest Allen Connally(architect for the project), Monsignor Edmund Venverloh, and Mrs. Harry B. Mathews, Jr.(President of the Colonial Dames in the State of Missouri and benefactor of the Bolduc restoration).

AT RIGHT: Charles Peterson lunches with members of the Colonial Dames during a return visit to Ste. Genevieve in the 1980s. Founder of the Historic American Buildings Survey, Peterson had documented the Bolduc House and several other significant historic buildings in Ste. Genevieve in the 1930s. He is joined by(from left) Ann Bodine, a tour guide, Virgie Stange and Margaret Mathews Jenks.

Pioneer Preservationists

A number of individuals played huge roles in the early days of preservation of Ste. Genevieve's architectural treasures. Norbert and Frankye Donze restored the Amoureux House, the Green Tree Tavern, the Vital St. Gemme Beauvais House and the Felix Rozier House (now the Inn St. Gemme Beauvais).

Norbert and Frankye Donze

"They were pioneer preservationists," said Lorraine Stange. "It seemed like after the Bolduc and the Amoureux, as more houses were opened and developed, people really found out that the outside world did want to come to Ste. Genevieve and that we had something worth displaying, preserving and using as educational tools."

Other individuals also made vital contributions by restoring significant historic structures. The Missouri Department of Natural Resources has also done a lion's share in the restoration and preservation of historic sites. As of 1998 the DNR and Site Administrator Jim Baker oversaw the Felix Valle State Historic Site, the Mammy Shaw House, the Amoureux and the DeLassus-Kern Houses.

One lifelong Ste. Genevieve resident pointed out that the town's financial doldrums may actually have helped save many of the historic houses, as well. While most of the surviving structures were built by the town's affluent colonial residents, they were often later occupied by less well-to-do families as the nineteenth and twentieth centuries wore on. Many had little choice but to keep their old houses patched together, thus preserving a relic which may otherwise have been destroyed if finances had allowed.

It is difficult to calculate how many of Ste. Genevieve's historic structures might have been demolished had it not been for the intervention of Lucille Basler. Basler, more than any other citizen of her day, dug into the history of the town and helped awaken people to the unique and fragile history the town possessed. The author of four books on the town's history, its houses and founding families, she helped found the imminently important Foundation for Restoration of Ste. Genevieve, Inc., and was a long-time officer. She also pushed legislation through the city government in the 1960s forming a Landmarks Commission to safeguard the historic structures downtown. For her efforts, Basler received the Gordon Gray Award from the National Trust for Historic Preservation in 1977 and has received numerous other honors and accolades.

"Lucille was virtually alone in teaching the Ste. Genevieve heritage to a generation of school children," Franzwa pointed out. "Without Lucille Basler, Frankye Donze, Vera Okenfuss, Fran Ballinger and several of the other early promoters of Ste. Genevieve, many of us who came later would not have come at all. They kept the flame burning for a long time and they deserve to be honored for this."

Lucille Basler

"She was a one-of-a-kind mover and shaker," Stange said. "She was very instrumental in organizing the Foundation for Restoration of Ste. Genevieve and she certainly contributed to the Foundation acquiring the Guibourd-Vallé House. She was urging people to wake up to what was in Ste. Genevieve. She was always beating a drum for Ste. Genevieve when I think some people just took for granted what we had here."

The tourism movement began to gain momentum during the 1960s, as more homes were restored and opened to the public. Since then the business community has developed some outstanding bed and breakfast establishments and restaurants, as well as a number of excellent antique and craft shops, to go along with the tour houses. The 1989 opening of the Great River Road Interpretive Center, designed by Jack Luer, was a major boon to the tourist trade. By riverboat, by charter bus, by car, and—beginning in 1997—by bicycle along the Mississippi River Trail, visitors were coming to see the old town.

In 1967, Greg Franzwa, a public relations executive-turned author, put out the first edition of *The Story of Old Ste. Genevieve.* It has recently entered its sixth edition and has shaped the way two generations of readers have perceived historic Ste. Genevieve.

Author Greg Franzwa at book signing at the Linden House

"He's one of the dearest friends Ste. Genevieve has ever had," Stange said. "That little book has done more to advertise Ste. Genevieve than any one thing. He was the first recipient of the Foundation's distinguished service award. No one deserved it more."

He has gained an even greater reputation as an expert on the Oregon and Sante Fe Trails. Franzwa also encouraged Ekberg, an Illinois State University professor, to continue his research in the early 1980s and published Ekberg's breakthrough *Colonial Ste. Genevieve* in 1985. It generated the most local discussion for challenging many of the oral traditions of local history, but also painted a wonderfully intricate portrait of everyday life in colonial Ste. Genevieve.

AT LEFT: The Ste. Genevieve Museum, constructed for the town's 1935 Bicentennial, is home to artifacts from the town's history. For a time, after its completion, it also housed the library.
BELOW: The Great River Road Interpretive Center, located at the corner of Main and Market, orients visitors to the history of the area.

One of Misselhorn's many pencil sketches shows the Fleur-de-lis Kindergarten which once stood on the northwest corner of Second and Market Streets. The building was once the home of François Lalumondiere. In the 1930s, it housed visiting art students of the Ste. Genevieve Art Colony. It was demolished in 1966 for the construction of Stanton-Wood Mortuary. The artist made this sketch in 1951.

Another dear friend of the community was revered Sparta, Illinois artist Roscoe Misselhorn. The artist, who died in 1997, sketched virtually every historic building and street scene in Ste. Genevieve. Most of his popular charcoal sketches were done in the 1940s and 1950s. A permanent display of his work is in the Misselhorn Gallery in the Great River Road Interpretive Center. He left another large collection of sketches to the city of Ste. Genevieve after his death.

Mr. and Mrs. Roscoe Misselhorn with a visitor during the dedication of the Great River Road Interpretive Center and Misselhorn Gallery.

250 Years

Paul Morice leads Ste. Genevieve's La Guignolée in the 250th Parade

A CELEBRATION OF TIME

ABOVE: Mary Rozier Sharp, Queen of the 1935 Bicentennial, returns 50 years later to take her place of honor in the 250th Parade. BELOW: Ste. Genevieve's 1985 Royalty

The town came together once again in 1985 to celebrate its 250th anniversary. This was at a time when Ste. Genevieve's traditional founding date of 1735 was being challenged. In keeping with the colloquialism of the community, resident Bernard Schram justified the celebration by commenting, "If it's inappropriate to celebrate a 250th, then we'll celebrate the 50th anniversary of the Bicentennial."

With contributions from businesses and organizations, a local "Fund for Progress" was established which hired a coordinator for the year-long celebration consisting of several weekend events.

At the King's Ball in February, a royal court was selected and a *Roi du Bal* was crowned. Ray "Schnay" Basler and his wife, Jeannette, would serve as the town's ambassadors for the forthcoming events. A Mass of Thanksgiving, celebrated by Archbishop John May, and a large parade officially kicked off the year in May. The grand prize float was awarded to the

ABOVE: Painting Ste. Genevieve's "Mural on the Wall"
BELOW: A Scottish band performs in the Sandbar

Ste. Genevieve County Pork Producers. Mary Rozier Sharp, who held the honor of being queen in 1935, returned to town to take her place in the parade as did committee members of the 225th anniversary.

A playwriting contest was sponsored which resulted in the premier production of "A Celebration of Time" at the newly restored Orris Theatre.

A wine fest was held on the Knights of Columbus lawn in June. Missouri vinters, including the town's own Ste. Genevieve Winery, offered their vintages to samplers of the fruit of the vine. The Knights' famous "pinchos" pork kabobs, made their debut that weekend and have become a tradition at their food stand each year during Jour de Fête.

A frontier rendezvous was held in Père Marquette City Park. Attracting black powder riflemen and folklorists who donned the garb of 18th century settlers, the event gave visitors the opportunity to step back to a time when trappers and traders came together to barter their wares and swap tales of the frontier.

The play "The Quilters" was performed by the Ste. Genevieve Council of Performing Arts. The play traced the rigors of frontier life symbolized in the patchwork of a beautiful quilt designed by Dorothy Huber. The play was complimented by a huge quilt show in the Valle Gymnasium—appropriate events in a community with a strong tradition of quilting.

Although the 250th celebration did not leave anything quite as substantial as the Museum—a lasting feature from the 1935 Bicentennial—it did sponsor the painting of the Mural on the Wall on the side of the Rozier Store building. The mural, designed by St. Louis artist Bob Fishbone, depicts the early settlers of Ste. Genevieve.

AT RIGHT: "The Quilters" performed by the Ste. Gen. Council of Performing Arts

OPPOSITE PAGE: Scenes from a frontier Rendezvous held in Père Marquette Park. Roasting game on a spit. Marv "The Colonel" Hilligoss leads militia through camp. Fr. Greg Schmidt distributes communion at Mass in the park.

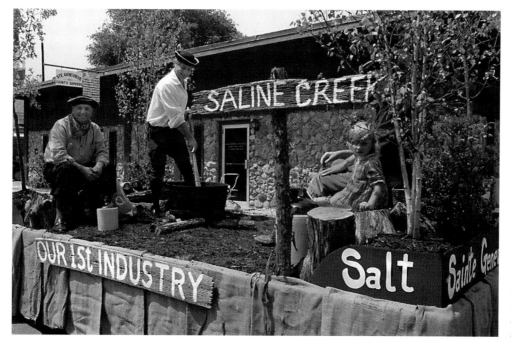

Celebrating Ste. Genevieve's first industry –salt– in the 250th Parade.

49

The year's festivities officially came to a close with the burial of a time capsule containing artifacts and memorabilia of the years events. These included a scroll containing signatures of many of the town's residents. A plaque, which marks the burial site at the west wall of the Museum, instructs descendants to unearth the capsule in the year 2085.—*bn*

AT RIGHT: The Hogenmiller brothers entertain during the Wine Fest.
BELOW: Harold Uding and Hope Hoffmeister serve samplings of Ste. Genevieve wine to interested wine tasters.

AT LEFT: Archbishop John May greets Knights of Columbus members at the 250th Ceremonial Mass.
BELOW: Musicians Win and Paul Grace entertain at the 250th Rendezvous.

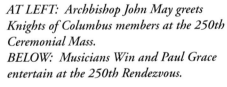

The Next Chapter

Each of Ste. Genevieve's anniversarial celebrations–1885, 1935, and1985–brought with them a flush of renewed excitement about the town and an eagerness to share it with the outside world.

Publications such as *Rozier's History of the Early Settlement of the Mississippi Valley*, Yealy's *Ste. Genevieve, The Story of Missouri's Oldest Settlement*, Franzwa's *The Story of Old Ste. Genevieve* and Ekberg's *Colonial Ste. Genevieve, An Adventure on the Mississippi Frontier*, touted Ste. Genevieve to an expanding population of historically-inclined readers.

In the last half of the twentieth century, other events have drawn attention to and shaped the Ste. Genevieve of today.

The 1980s Great River Road Project gave Ste. Genevieve a face-lift with its old-style street lamps, pebbled sidewalks, tree plantings and interpretive history center. Enhanced with its new "old town" look, tourists as well as locals have been drawn to stroll her streets and notice her treasures.

The creation in 1983 of an organization known as the Center for French Colonial Studies has established a dialogue among representatives of the various French settlements along the Mississippi River from French Canada to New Orleans. As a member of this group, Ste. Genevieve's historic significance has been highlighted among the academic community.

The world of highschool sports took note of Ste. Genevieve when, in two different years, it earned the state-wide moniker as "Title Town." This first happened in 1980 when the Ste. Gen. Headhunters and the Valle Lady Warriors both won Missouri State Volleyball championships in their classes. Again, in 1992, the two school's football teams, the Dragons and the Warriors, won state championships. By 1998, Valle had claimed a whopping nine state football championships.

No contest in Ste. Genevieve's history, however, would bring it to the forefront as did the flood of 1993, when the media lavished attention on the town as it fought to win the battle against the mighty Mississippi.

Ste. Genevieve was put on the map in the homes of viewers worldwide. The success of the battle, however, was not as well known as the fight itself, and tourism suffered in its aftermath, with many believing Ste. Genevieve to have been swept away by the floodwaters. In the wake of the flood, construction began in 1997 on a federal levee to protect the town— primarily because of its historic significance. However, some downtown businesses, having moved to the safety of the expanding west side of town, remained there after the flood threat was gone.

This migration westward was not new. It had begun following World War II with the residential development of the International Addition. With streets named after some of Ste. Genevieve's historical characters–Audubon, Scott, Austin, LaRose and Linn–the addition was the direct result of an effort to provide returning veterans with employment. For $500 one could enter a lottery for a lot in the proposed residential district. The proceeds of the sale went to constructing a building (now Biltbest Windows) to house International Shoe Company which was willing to come to Ste. Genevieve if the city could provide it with a suitable building.

The westward push continued and what had once been farm and pastureland with just an occasional service station along old Hwy. 25 (now U.S. 61) had begun in 1970 to take on the look of "Anytown, USA" with its fast food restaurants and strip mall. With the construction of a community center building in 1999 and an industrial park area, Ste. Genevieve's westward expansion is pushing even farther.

As Ste. Genevieve enters the new millennium, it faces some hard questions such as how best to preserve its history and character, and at the same time plan for its growth and secure its future. The decisions made will certainly reflect the wisdom or folly of its leaders today for the next chapter in Ste Genevieve's history. *—mle, psn, bn*

A Stroll Down Memory Lane

*John and Sophie Basler,
founders of Basler Funeral Home,
one of Ste. Genevieve's century-old family-run businesses.*

*A contingent of willing workers prepares to spread creek gravel on a
dirt-lined Main Street in front of the Presbyterian Church.*

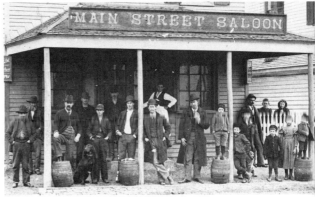

The Moreau Homeplace

Patrons of the Main Street Saloon at Washington Street

Naumann's Butcher Shop on Merchant St.

Okenfuss Hardware

A group of local thespians take to the footlights.

John L. Boverie General Merchandise on Third St.

The 1949 Lion's Club

The 1937 Ste. Genevieve Indians

Jockie Baumgartner accepts the keys to Ste. Genevieve's first police car (a 1950 Oldsmobile) from K.O. Barley.

ABOVE: Bob Okenfuss(left), Cap Donze and Dolph Okenfuss enjoy a cold one at the Palace Bar as Robert "Beans" Sexauer looks on.
BELOW: A young Jerry Meyer, in full cowboy attire, poses by a sign of the Standard Gas Station at the corner of Main and Merchant.

ABOVE: Slim Rogers and the KSGM Blue Denim Boys
BELOW: A 1937 panorama of the Elder Manufacturing employees

The Janis-Ziegler House, commonly known as the Green Tree Tavern, one of the oldest surviving structures in town, stands prominently overlooking the area once known as Ziegler Falls on the South Gabouri Creek in this late-19th Century photograph. The terrain around the house has been altered dramatically since the time of this photo. When the St. Mary Road was widened, the rock wall lining the creek, was buried. More recently, following the flood of 1993, the road was raised to provide protection against future flooding, burying the stone wall at the base of the house.

—Missouri Historical Society photo

Poteaux en terre

Today the United States has only five authentic surviving examples of the most popular French Creole building practice, poteaux en terre or posts-in-the-ground construction. The French drove or buried hand-hewn red cedar logs directly into the earth to form both the foundation and walls. Three of the five surviving buildings stand proudly in remote Ste.Genevieve. The other two are in Natchitoches, Louisiana and Pascagoula, Mississippi. These historic homes have withstood the New Madrid earthquakes, several major floods, and the constant threats of potential termite damage and rot, to span two centuries and give the town a place in history.

Amoureux House

Bequette-Ribault House

Vital St.Gemme Beauvais House

The Bolduc House, Bolduc-LeMeilleur and the Jean Baptiste Vallé House line Main Street—La Grande Rue of early Ste. Genevieve

ARCHITECTURE

Perhaps a New Englander would shrug at the significance of Ste. Genevieve's 200-year-old houses. Certainly many lifelong residents of the town tend to overlook them. For a visiting Midwesterner, however—or anyone who can appreciate fine old structures that combine architectural significance and aesthetic charm—the city is magic.

Simply put, quiet, unassuming Ste. Genevieve has something that virtually no one else in North America has—an authentic collection of carefully restored eighteenth (and early nineteenth) century structures, built in the traditional French Creole fashion. Five *poteaux en terre*, or "post-in-the-ground" houses exist in the United States. Three of the five are in Ste. Genevieve.

"People are surprised to learn that Ste.Genevieve has more authentic French Colonial structures than New Orleans," noted Dr. Osmund Overby of the University of Missouri, "but that is a fact."

Overby led a University of Missouri team that took part in the HABS (Historic American Buildings Survey) project of the 1980s. Along with him, Dr. Richard Guyette performed dendrochronology (tree ring) borings on some two dozen key Ste. Genevieve buildings. Together they determined that many of the historic buildings were not quite as old as originally thought, although some scholars take issue with some of the study's findings. Still, an amazing number of structures are standing that were here before Missouri joined the Union in 1821. Many of those have either undergone very minimal changes or have been lovingly restored.

In fact, HABS founder Charles Peterson stated in 1997 that due to the tragic loss of many of the French Colonial structures he photographed in Canada in the 1930s, Ste. Genevieve can legitimately be called the leading French Colonial architecture collection in North America. Of course, the French Colonial structures are not the only historic gems in Ste. Genevieve. A stroller or motorist may take in an intriguing tapestry of architectural heritage, with virtually every major American style of the eighteenth, nineteenth and early twentieth centuries represented.

The Great Date Debate

To most professional historians, dendro-chronology has proven to be a very reliable science for dating historic structures. To some, it remains just "the 'D' word." Ste. Genevieve has been a battleground for the science and those who question it–usually owners or restorers of houses dated later than traditionally believed.

Ste. Genevieve stepped into the middle of the debate in the mid-1980s, when Dr. Richard P. Guyette of the University of Missouri–Columbia, did dendrochronology (or tree ring) studies of 24 historic houses here. His results were released in conjunction with an architectural survey done by Dr. Osmund Overby, also of the University of Missouri.

The results indicated that many of the town's historic structures were not as old as previously believed. That, coupled with the publication about that time of Carl Ekberg's *Colonial Ste. Genevieve*, has spawned more than a decade of debate.

Dendrochronology, the study of tree rings, originated in the American Southwest, where A.E. Douglass used the technique to date timbers in adobe dwellings in the 1910s. It has been successfully used in the eastern U.S. and in Europe. Tree rings preserve a record of a tree's annual growth. Variations in the ring patterns–including frost rings (rings with cambial damage caused by late spring frosts)–can be brought about by changes in climatic conditions. Since the trees in a general area experience a similar climate, the ring width patterns are similar and can be crossdated–put side-by-side and compared with "chronologies" of the same species.

"When someone doesn't accept a date, they often rationalize that the climate, which controls the similarity in tree rings is not the same in, say Ste. Genevieve as it is in St. Louis," Guyette stated recently. "Thus, how can you possibly use old oak trees from Babler State Park to date oak house timbers in Ste. Genevieve?

"The answer is that the climate does not have to be exactly the same, just similar from year to year. For instance, although there are many years in which climate is only weakly limiting to the growth of trees, there are other years such as 1952, 1936, 1780, 1784, 1735, 1604 ... during which most trees and species have narrow rings."

Other features such, as frost rings, are big clues. The years 1716, 1715 and 1704 were the only significant frost rings of the 18th century in the area. In the immediate Ste. Genevieve environ, the 1716 frost ring is particularly telling. The area climate also produced distinctive ring-width patterns or "signature years," such as narrow rings in 1735 and 1736. The period just before and after 1784 was distinctive for redcedar. The 1784 ring was nearly always narrow and 1783 wide. When one of these distinctive finger print-like rings is identified, it becomes a simple matter of counting years from that year until the cutting of the tree.

"The point is that although reference chronologies should be as close as possible, St. Louis is climatically very similar to Ste. Genevieve," Guyette continued. "Also, Ste. Genevieve house timbers may have well come from near St. Louis or beyond by river transport."

Samples are taken by boring small holes in pieces of wood. Guyette prefers using wall logs, floor beams, sills, plates, rafters and trusses, thus avoiding questions of new roofs or reused timbers. He took 375 samples from 24 houses in Ste. Genevieve County. Twenty were in the city of Ste. Genevieve. Definitive dates could not be placed on just four of the 24 houses due to deteriorated lumber and other problems.

Some critics question the reliability of the science–particularly its ability to accurately date ce-

The restored Bequette-Ribault House was the subject of intensive dendrochronology study in the 1980s.

dar. Jack Luer, who directed the restoration of the Bequette-Ribault and also worked on the Green Tree Tavern, Felix Vallé House and Amoureux House, doesn't believe the cedar dates.

"It's a very good, very thorough science," Luer said of dendrochronology. "Certain woods just cannot be dated. A lot of dates gotten with a piece of wood can be backed up with written documents of the period. They fit together very well. When you try to get into cedar, I've not been able to back up cedar dates with anything documented.

"You can have a cedar tree not throw any rings one year and another year it can throw two rings. When you have this kind of problem, people should not be putting all their eggs in one basket."

"Eastern redcedar has a tendency to double-ring if the weather is dry in the middle of the year," said Larry Grantham, an archeologist for the Division of State Parks for 18 years, who studied dendrochronology at the University of Missouri. "If you can match them up with oak dates, then you can probably accept the Eastern redcedar dates as reliable, too.

You've got to watch out a little with Eastern redcedar, but if Richard Guyette's got a good chronology for both oak and redcedar, I'd be relatively inclined to believe them–particularly if they're crossmatched."

Dendrochronologists agree that cedar can be challenging. They stress, though, that an experienced professional, with proper equipment, can find more than enough crossmatching redcedar.

"In some places in the world, redcedar doesn't cross date," Guyette said. "In fact, some cedar in Missouri doesn't cross-date—but for the most part it does. If it cross-dates we use it, if it doesn't, we don't."

Kiyomi Morino, a research specialist for five years at the highly-esteemed Laboratory for Tree Ring Research at the University of Arizona, observed that it takes some experience to read some of the more difficult redcedar samples.

"I recently looked at some Virginia redcedar. It was very difficult to cross-date because, in some cases, its rings were very narrow and had ring boundaries difficult to see," she related. "After looking at the wood and comparing it for a while and comparing different trees, though, I was able to see some cross-dating. These were trees that were basically growing out of the sides of cliffs, so growth was very slow and many of the rings were very narrow."

The aforementioned false rings are the biggest concern, but experts can weed those out, as well. "It absolutely can be dated," Guyette stressed. "It probably would present problems for an amateur, but in general, it shouldn't. We do get pieces of cedar that do not cross-date, but that's true of all of our species."

One of the main houses in contention is the Bequette-Ribault, tested by Guyette during Luer's restoration in 1984. The house, believed to have been built in the 1770s or 1780s, dated out to 1807 and 1808.

Due to the easy access to the logs, the co-operation of the owners, Royce and Marge Wilhauk, and surprise over the findings, Guyette dated a whopping 21 pieces of timber from the small *poteaux-en-terre* house. Eleven were redcedar wall logs, four white oak floor beams, one white oak truss member and window sill each and four shortpine floorboards. The trees, according to Guyette's findings, were all felled in 1807 or 1808—including the oak, which Luer agreed can be dated with "no sweat."

"Being placed in the position of a 'myth breaker' when a house turns out to be more recently built than thought, was emotionally wrenching," Guyette recalled. "The scientific method and independent replication by others allowed me to be objective about the dates." Dr. David Stahle of the University of Arkansas Tree Ring Laboratory provided independent verification of Guyette's dating on selected key samples later.

Fifty percent of the Bequette-Ribault's redcedar cross-dated (typical for the species in Missouri, according to Guyette), and 87 percent of the oak. People still disagree over the construction of the house, though.

Luer has documented the 60 or so authentic French Colonial homes left in the old Illinois Country in his book "The Vanishing French Heritage." He has his own possible theories as to the origin of the house. Among them is that it could have been a slave cabin belonging to Laurette Gabouri, as far back as the 1750s. Luer has done considerable research on the Beauvais and Bequette families, who owned the land after Gabouri.

He also questioned whether the building style of the house (as he, Jesse Francis and Dr. Melburn Thurman interpreted it during the restoration) fits in with what was already being built in the area by 1808.

"I'm not a historian, but I can read documentation other people have done," Luer said. "I think three of these buildings (Bequette-Ribault, Amoureux and Beauvais) have been badly misrepresented. "I think you've got to just put your opinion on it—you don't say 'It was definitely this.' I think these buildings need more investigation. I'm the first to tell you I need more research."

That research often leads to as many questions as answers. Land records are not always clear about the location or existence of a dwelling on a piece of property.

If further research does, indeed, lead scholars to form a different interpretation of Ste. Genevieve's history than what the findings of the 1980s provided, chances are it will create just as much controversy.

For the sake of consistency, this publication references the dating of the Historic American Buildings Survey and the dendrochronology studies of the 1980s and presents, when available, information which suggests dates other than those recorded in the HABS report.

As with any scholarly approach, an open mind and continued research are the best tools with which to unravel the mysteries yet to be uncovered in Ste. Genevieve's history. Those interested in a more detailed account of the history of Ste. Genevieve and its architecture would do well to consult any of the excellent resources listed in the bibliography at the back of this book and to conduct their own investigative research.

Spotlight on Restoration

The painstaking restoration of the Bequette-Ribault house was an excellent example of preservation in action. Neighbors watched as a community eyesore was stripped down to its vertical log shell and then transformed into the fine example that it is today. Archaeological digs were conducted by Mel Thurman to establish the location of the gallery porch posts of the original structure. Cedar timbers, cut from area woodlands, were hand-hewn using adz and drawknife by preservationist Jesse Francis to replace members that were beyond repair. Willows were cut from the Mississippi River bottoms to be used for the reconstruction of the roof rafters. The project was overseen by architect Jack Luer. The Bequette-Ribault restoration project gave architectural historians and preservationists a detailed look at French Creole construction practices of the late 1700s. Throughout the eight year project, meticulous documentation was made as architectural details were uncovered. Much of this has been documented in Thurman's 1984 publication "Building a House in 18th Century Ste. Genevieve."

The French Built Them To Last

Of the remaining French Creole structures in Ste. Genevieve, the three *poteaux en terre* or "posts in the ground" houses are perhaps the most intriguing to architectural historians. Because of its simple design and ease of construction, this was the most common method of building among the colonial French, yet only five examples survive in North America today. *Poteaux sur solle,* or "posts on a sill" was another popular French Creole method and many survive of these.

Some are impressively restored or in the process of restoration, and many lie disguised beneath clapboard or siding with their rooflines unrecognizably altered.

The gradual exodus from the old townsite to the new was begun by the less affluent residents, Ekberg's research suggests. By 1790 cedar was considerably more expensive than oak and other woods. Therefore, a poor man was not in a position to use the seemingly indestructible wood. It is likely that the first houses constructed in the new town were small, less carefully constructed cabins or shacks, made of oak and other less durable woods. Those seem to have long since vanished.

It was when the wealthy merchants, planters and other local elite began to give up on their larger investments in the old town, that the face of the new town was permanently stamped. As men like Louis Bolduc, Nicolas and François Janis, Vital St. Gemme Beauvais and the Vallé brothers used their wealth and their slave man-power to construct well-built homes in the early 1790s, an architectural legacy was left that would make tiny Ste. Genevieve unique in North America and help give it the designation as a National Historic Landmark District some 200 years later.

(Background photo) A diorama of French Colonial Ste. Genevieve housed in the Old Courthouse in St. Louis. Settled in the mid-1700s, the French in Ste. Genevieve represented one of the major European powers vying for the vast territory west of the Mississippi River. The French first built their homes in the alluvial plains of the river valley just south of present day Ste. Genevieve and later in the river hills where the town is now. Several of the early French vertical log homes still stand. This diorama and others housed in the Old Courthouse were built in the 1940s as part of the WPA program of the post-Depression years. (Inset) A cutaway model of a French Creole vertical log house on display at the Old Courthouse in St. Louis.

Janis-Ziegler House

According to tree ring studies, the Janis-Ziegler House, better known as the Green Tree Tavern, was the first of the surviving homes constructed. Either the aging Nicolas Janis or his son François had the immensely important building constructed in 1790 or 1791. In fact, Guyette suggested in his report, "Tree Ring Dating of French Colonial Vertical Log Houses in Ste. Genevieve, Missouri," that it is not only Ste. Genevieve's oldest building, but "possibly the oldest structure in the state of Missouri." It has been undergoing an extensive period of study and restoration by new owner Professor Hilliard Goldman and architectural historian Jack Luer. Guyette believes that early in its life (about 1808), the Green Tree was enlarged and received one of the city's several remarkable trusses. The truss collar and rafters are of pine, the older floor beams of white oak. The Green

During its restoration in the late-1990s, the vertical log construction of the Green Tree Tavern was readily visible when the lathe was stripped from its exterior.

The 200-year-old Green Tree Tavern sits in Mississippi floodwater in August 1993.

Tree's greatest claim to fame came after the U.S. took over the territory. It became the first tavern in the Louisiana Territory and was later the first tobacco store in the U.S. west of the Mississippi, as well as supposedly being the first Masonic meeting hall west of the Mississippi.

Goldman and Luer disproved legends of a hiding place existing inside the triangular fire place, where the Janis family supposedly intended to hide in case of Osage attack. They did, however, uncover the name "Janis," very regally carved into the wood when they uncovered one *galerie* pillar. Another pillar displayed a Masonic emblem, seeming to support the house's Masonic tradition. The carvings had to have been made before 1844, when the red cedar pillars were covered with wood siding.

The grand old building was restored as a tourist attraction in the 1960s by the Donzes, but was the one key historic structure that suffered severe damage during the 1993 flood. For some three months, the 200-year-old building sat in up to eighteen inches of murky flood water. It was on the cover of *Damaged and Threatened National Historic Landmarks 1993 Report,* a national publication, put out by the National Park Service. The *galerie* porch was largely destroyed and an investor with infinite patience and resources was needed to restore the *poteaux sur solle* beauty. Goldman, a history professor at St. Louis Community College at Meramec, has been at work on the old structure since 1996.

The Green Tree was open to the public as a tour house in the 1960s and 70s. Among its many attractions were the triple fireplaces(two pictured here) which shared one common flue.

Bolduc House Museum

When visitors ask directions to "the old house," everyone knows which one they mean—even those locals who don't know its name. It is, of course, the Louis Bolduc House, handsomely restored by Dr. Ernest Allen Connally into an eye-popping gem. The old *poteaux sur solle* house had not undergone terribly extensive modernization over the years and Connally's skillful hand guided the final phases of a long and patient restoration process. He took heat in some quarters for the attractive stone kitchen (the only historic recreation in town) and the gorgeous, evenly-matched stockade fence. Informed of the criticism, he quipped to Estel Smith, construction foreman for Mississippi Lime at the time and later a popular *Ste. Genevieve Herald* columnist that "we were under no obligation to build ugly" in the name of historical accuracy.

This is one of several houses rumored for years to have been moved from the old town site and reassembled. Experts from Peterson to Connally to Guyette to Ekberg debunk this theory. It seems apparent, however, that at least the white oak ceiling timber of the south side of the house was indeed salvaged from the old town. "Composed solely of squared timbers with all the sap-wood removed... indicates this

ceiling was moved from the old town," Guyette suggested. Bolduc had a house built in 1770—the construction contract survives. The ceiling timbers may have come from it. One wall log strangely dated to 1788 while all other samples came back 1792 and 1793. Perhaps this log was from a post-flood repair job on the 1770 structure following one of the great floods of the 1780s and was still salvageable in 1792. In any case, the Bolduc boasts some of the oldest pieces of lumber in town.

Connally's restoration work on the Bolduc was of international significance. It marked one of the first times a structure had been restored for its architectural rather than historical significance.

"I think it's a major event in the understanding and appreciation of French Colonial architecture," Overby said of Connally and his work on the Bolduc. "He has been widely recognized for it and very deservedly. It was a very thorough restoration and does a wonderful job of recreating that setting for the lives of at least the wealthy people in Ste. Genevieve in the eighteenth century."

"We were under no obligation to build ugly."

"It's a document," Connally said in a 1997 interview. "Part of its function is to help us remember. That makes it a link with the past in material culture—a direct link, tangible and true."

Operated by The National Society of The Colonial Dames of America in the State of Missouri, the Bolduc House Museum is now a tour house, authentically decorated with austere period furnishings. Among them is a large armoire with a water stain running about two feet above

the floor. The piece is believed to have survived the flood of 1785 in the old town. The date "1735" has been carved inside it, but appears to be a twentieth century inscription.

Connally, who went on to serve as associate director of the National Park Service, had a simple formula in restoring the grand old house. "In the Bolduc I simply had to let the building itself tell me what it was," he said. "There were very few documentary records of any kind about the house. We had to depend on the building itself. It provided all the evidence we needed."

The Bolduc enjoys the status of being the only building in Ste. Genevieve designated as a National Historic Landmark.

Visitors to the Bolduc House find a total restoration. The impressive creole structure, furnished with period pieces, is complimented by the surrounding grounds which include a colonial garden complete with grape arbor and herbs.

"In the Bolduc, I simply had to let the building itself tell me what it was."

Bolduc-LeMeilleur House

Next to the Bolduc is the restored French creole vernacular heavy timber frame Bolduc-LeMeilleur, circa 1820. It is best remembered as the Sisters of Loretto Convent and Detchemendy House hotel. Connally also directed its controversial restoration, which included the razing of the connected brick store building

from the same period. The public saw the old convent reduced to the shell of the original structure before being rebuilt to its present state. The LeMeilleur is operated by The National Society of The Colonial Dames in the State of Missouri along with the Bolduc House Museum and the circa 1811 Linden House across South Main Street.

A small group of gardeners gather beneath the immense linden tree across from the Bolduc House to share ideas for retiring their gardens in the fall.

Gemien Beauvais/Linden House

The Gemien Beauvais or Linden House, directly across Main from the Bolduc House, is the third structure along *La Grande Rue* owned and operated by The National Society of The Colonial Dames in the State of Missouri. The original timber frame structure, c.1811, has been modified and enlarged several times giving the building its present look. The house gets its common name from the immense linden tree which graces the property.(See photo, previous page).

The Linden House is open to the public on special occasions such as the Christmas Walk, candlelight tours, and informational herb programs.

Vital St. Gemme Beauvais House

One block north of the Linden House is the Vital St. Gemme Beauvais House. It is significant for more than one reason. First, it is one of the three *poteaux en terre* houses in town. Secondly, it is among the oldest, the south half of the house dating to about 1792. Finally, it was here that young Henry Marie Brackenridge received his crash course in French language and civilization. (See story, p.12) Brackenridge left considerable written documentation about the house, the Beauvais family and the town in general. The house's history did not fade in significance after the colonial period, though. It has always housed important local leaders. In 1848 Louis C. Menard, who would later serve as mayor, bought the house. He was a son of Illinois statesman Pierre Menard. His wife, Augustine, was the great-granddaughter of Vital St.

Gemme Beauvais, and in the late 1800s was considered the town's leading historian along with her younger brother, Captain Gustavus St. Gemme. Through the years, the house has served as the beloved home to many and for a short time in the 1980s was open to the public as a tour house with an outstanding heirloom garden in back.

Unlike many of the colonial homes in Ste. Genevieve, the Beauvais has a mixture of *pierrotage*–stone and lime mortar–between the ancient vertical logs. Most of the homes of this era used *bouzillage*–a mixture of clay, chopped straw, animal hair and basically whatever the builder could find.

The house, though never directly affected by the floods, has sat empty for a number of years awaiting restoration after the completion of the federal levee.

Jean Baptiste Vallé House

Located at the northwest corner of Main and Market Streets is the important Jean Baptiste Vallé House. Owned by only three families, the great house was modified extensively in the mid-1800s. It was purchased around 1865 by Leon Vion, a native of France. His great-granddaughter Vion Papin Schram and her husband Bernard have lived there more than thirty years. Constructed in 1794, the house clearly marked the affluent part of the new town—that area now consisting of South Main (then called *La Grande Rue*), South Gabouri Street and Market Street (*Rue à l'Eglise*). To the south was Louis Bolduc's large lot which was bordered on its south side by Jean Baptiste Pratte's property. François Vallé II owned a large lot extending from Pratte's western line to Second Street. Across *La Grande Rue* and to the south of J.B. Vallé, Jean Baptiste Moreaux constructed a home(where the Linden House now stands). Vital St. Gemme Beauvais was one block to the north of Moreaux. Estimating the locations of the new town's primary homes during its first decade of existence is fascinating to contemplate.

Vion Papin Schram in her garden.

The J. B. Vallé House is an eye-catching relic, graced by a colonial-style garden and wooden fence, keeping largely intact the colonial flavor of the historic district. A circa-1812 barn on the lot was destroyed by a storm in the 1970s and was replaced by a combination shed-garage which strongly resembles the original structure.

The basement is made of four-feet thick rubblestone, with three-quarter-round masonry buttresses. The design of basement led to persistent rumors that it had been used as a fort prior to the house itself standing on the spot. Historians today doubt this. The basement seems to suggest that the grand old house was constructed in three different stages.

As a writer and public relations person, Bernie Schram and his wife Vion have been host to many scholars, historians, and VIPs. Vion, a fine French cook, has a long-standing reputation for creating culinary works of art out of eggs—once gathered from her own hen house—and asparagus, peas, lettuces, and other vegetables and fruits grown in her own garden. Their wine cellar has a reputation of its own, and the wine made from the fruits of their vineyard has gladdened the spirits of many so fortunate to be entertained by the couple. In a great sense, they have brought to life the French hospitality and the diplomatic skills long associated with the home's original owners and family.

Amoureux House

At the same time that "New Ste. Genevieve" or *les petites côtes* was emerging, New Bourbon was founded, two miles to the south, atop the bluff overlooking *le grand champ*. A county road still bears its name. Populated by a group of French monarchists—some with noble blood lines—the village was a large and viable community during the colonial era, but completely gone by the 1840s. A row of homes stretched from the new town of Ste. Genevieve to New Bourbon along what are now St. Marys Road and US Highway 61. A handful of these old structures survive. In fact, it is here that the other two *poteaux en terre* structures still stand.

The Amoureux House, built about 1792, was long said to have been occupied by Mathurin Michel Amoureux, a French nobleman. He came to America in 1793 after corresponding with a young Thomas Jefferson, apparently seeking Jefferson's view on revolution, as strife ripped Bourbon France apart.

Personnel of the Department of Natural Resources, who now controls the property, have concluded that the house probably did not enter the Amoureux family until 1852, when it was purchased by Mathurin's youngest son, Benjamin. It is now believed that the house was originally built by Jean Baptiste St. Gemme Beauvais, a brother of Vital St. Gemme Beauvais.

Some of its original posts-in-the-ground were damaged after the basement was flooded for part of the summer of 1993 and had to be stabilized. Purchased by the French Heritage Relief Committee (founded by author/historian Charles Balesi) shortly thereafter, it was donated to the State of Missouri as part of the state historic site in Ste. Genevieve. The gift of the house also led to the creation of a vitally important organization called *Les Amis* (the friends), a St. Louis-based group that supports French heritage, including Ste. Genevieve's unique French architecture.

The Amoureux and Bequette-Ribault houses have a unique bond. The Bequette-Ribault came into the possession of "Clarise, a free woman of color," who was brought to Ste. Genevieve from Virginia by John Ribault, a wealthy French widower. Clarise purchased the house in 1837 and raised her children by Ribault, after his death.

The Bequette-Ribault House becomes more significant in that it is one of only a handful of surviving houses owned by a black woman in a slave state prior to the Civil War. By all accounts, Clarise Ribault was accepted as graciously as any white widow would have been, raising her mulatto children after Ribault died. The house remained in the Ribault family until the last grandson died in 1969.

The Amoureux family, too, started a mulatto tradition in the grand old house. According to Leola Amoureux Duckett in *The Amoureux Family Of Ste. Genevieve*, Mathurin's son Benjamin (1796-1878) fell madly in love with the daughter of a low class white family. Mathurin did not approve and

A mulatto family poses on the porch of one of Ste. Genevieve's creole houses. (Identities not known.)

forbade them to marry. Supposedly to spite his father, young Benjamin instead married Pelagie Vital, a mulatress owned by Vital St. Gemme Beauvais. "Benjamin and Pelagie, in the dead of the night, rowed across the river in a small boat to Illinois, where they found a priest to marry them," Duckett wrote. "It was alleged that Benjamin purchased his wife and their 16-month-old son, Felix, from the Beauvais' widow on the eleventh day of June, 1832." Throughout the nineteenth century, the Amoureux and Ribault families lived as neighbors, apparently not experiencing much, if any prejudice. Ste. Genevieve had a largely non-racist mentality during the eighteenth and early nineteenth centuries.

Bequette-Ribault House

Not far down St. Marys Road is the historic Bequette-Ribault House. The "little jewel," as current owner Donna Card Charron calls it, has been at the center of the historical dating controversy for well over a decade. Long believed to have been built in the 1770s, tree ring tests by Guyette consistently came back with dates of 1807 and 1808. This was true both of red cedar (which some architectural historians feel is difficult to date accurately, see story, p. 58) and oak samples. The tests were done in the mid-1980s during an extensive restoration by owners Royce and Marge Wilhauk who cite documentation which they believe dates the house c.1785.

The Wilhauks operated the house as a living history museum where school groups and history students could get a hands-on experience of colonial life, some even camping out in the restored dwelling. To complement the project, the Wilhauks relocated the Durand cabin—another vertical log structure—to the Ribault property. To secure the

historic value and aesthetic appearance of their labors, the Wilhauks sold the property to the Department of Natural Resources with covenants that any future buyers would have to abide by.

Their enthusiasm for the history of the area is also manifest in their own "Creole House" private residence which they operate as a bed and breakfast. Designed by architect Jack Luer in the French Creole tradition, the impressive building sits on a hill just behind the Bequette-Ribault overlooking *le grand champ*.

Pierre Dorlac House

Another significant colonial structure on St. Mary Road is the Pierre Dorlac House. By the first decade of the nineteenth century, Ste. Genevieve culture was changing and so were architectural patterns. Overby uses the Dorlac House (circa 1807) as an example of "the coexistence of American and Creole construction practices." Remodeled early in the nineteenth century to fit the Greek Revival craze, the attractive house is significant for another reason. The white oak floor beams and short pine ceiling joists show traces of mineralization. Guyette believes this indicates they were floated downriver to Ste. Genevieve. Although

it bears the name of Pierre Dorlac, Jean Baptiste Vallé II was known to have owned the house as well.

François Vallé II House

Adz marks are evident in the squaring of the attic timbers of the François Vallé II house. The heavy timbers rest on the top plate of the vertical log walls of this poteaux sur solle *structure.*

When François Vallé II made the decision to move from the original townsite of Ste. Genevieve to the new town in the late 1700s, it marked one of the final death knells for the old community. His home (now a private residence) at 167 South Gabouri Street has had some of its structural members altered (the roof rafters are a late-nineteenth century modification with none of the original trusswork remaining) but the vertical log walls remain intact behind clapboard siding. Heavy joists in the ceiling, some measuring 10 inches on a side, span the length of the original structure. Notches cut in some of these members are located at irregular intervals and could suggest their having been used in some other structure. The house is a prime example of Ste. Genevieve's many unrestored, yet architecturally significant structures which have stood the test of time beneath decades of clapboard and paint.

Unraveling the DeLassus-Kern Mystery

The old Kern farm house, two miles south of town on U.S. Highway 61, has been the subject of in-depth investigation and speculation since the 1980s. At that time a six-room vertical log structure was discovered inside the aging farm house. Dendrochronology indicated the logs, hand hewn and put together in traditional French Creole style, were from trees felled in 1793. That was the year a house was built for French nobleman Pierre Charles DeHault DeLassus DeLuziere. The *chevalier* and his family had fled the guillotine of the French Revolution. He arrived in New Bourbon in 1793 and immediately became commandant. His son Charles would soon become lieutenant governor of the Louisiana Territory. One of the best-educated and most influential men in the region, DeLassus was a key figure in the colonial era.

Excitement arose among scholarly ranks as the sagging late nineteenth century farm house began to go by the moniker "DeLuziere-Kern House," with the belief that the six-room vertical log section must have been the *chevalier's* six-room vertical log house. It was, after all, built on land that had clearly belonged to DeLassus.

A problem soon arose in that theory. Maps emerged from noted cartographer Nicolas de Finiels, who did a detailed map of the region for the Spanish government in the 1790s. While it verified that DeLassus owned the land in question, it clearly marked his residence on a hill, well back of the plane where the current structure sits. Finiels and others also made reference to his home sitting atop a hill, commanding a splendid view.

The house was donated to the state of Missouri after it was damaged by the 1993 flood. The Department of Natural Resources took control of the property in the mid-1990s and began a careful investigation. Some experts, like Ekberg, argued all along that it was a case of mistaken identity.

It remained for Dr. Kit Wesler of Murray State (Ky.) University and Professors Carol Morrow and Bonnie Stepenoff of Southeast Missouri State University, and their archaeology students to solve the mystery in 1997. Wesler, Morrow and Stepenoff finished the 1997 archaeology field school convinced that the original six-room section of the house (the second floor was added around 1890) was not on its current location before 1830. Wesler based this finding partly on archaeological evidence. No trace of pre-1820 pottery was found on the site—everything found was either Indian or later nineteenth century. The students, under Stepenoff and Morrow's guidance, also unearthed a paper trail that helped explain what may have happened. DeLassus died in 1806, but the property remained in the family into the 1830s. The current house site was bought in 1834 by Andrew Swank, known to be a local land developer. Swank, a distant relative, paid $200 for the land. He was known to be buying up new and used timber and to be conducting a number of land deals during the decade. Three years later, in 1837, he sold the same lot for a whopping $1200. This seems to give major credence to Wesler's assertion that Swank likely disassembled the DeLassus house on the hill between those years and reassembled it beneath the bluff. Whether it was carefully reassembled in its original fashion or whether it merely contained some components from the *chevalier's* house is not known.

An 1866 newspaper article, in which land owner John Kern seemingly pointed toward the nearby hill when speaking of the "Frenchman" who built the house, added to the case. So did the production of some late eighteenth century pottery pieces, found atop the hill, where the current land owner had unearthed them. Wesler hopes to get an opportunity to do archaeology work on the hill in the future. The house is still the only existing physical connection with New Bourbon and is an interesting blending of French and German building styles.

Guibourd-Vallé House

In some ways the Guibourd-Valle might be called the last major French Creole house in Ste. Genevieve—even though the building style survived into the middle of the nineteenth century. This may explain how it was long thought to have been built as early as 1784. Numerous pieces of documentation and tree ring borings now suggest it having been constructed in 1806. A large, well-maintained example of the French Creole *poteaux sur solle* house, the Guibourd-Valle employs the traditional French vertical, hewn log (white oak) structural system, mortised into a sill, infilled with *bouzillage* and plastered or sheathed with horizontal clapboards. The *galerie* survives on front and back, the back having been enclosed in the 1930s. At one time the *galerie* was thought to encircle the entire house.

The roof trusses of the Guibourd-Vallé are readily accessible to the public in the attic of the historic old home.

Jacques Guibourd, a wealthy French-born Santo Dominigon planter, barely escaped the Santo Domingo slave uprising with his life. He supposedly was smuggled out of the country in a barrel by a loyal slave, Moros. Although tradition has had Guibourd arriving in Ste. Genevieve quite well-to-do, his son Omar painted quite a different picture of his arrival in an 1825 excerpt from his diary, published in the *Missouri Historical Society Bulletin* in 1952. According to Omar Guibourd, his father fled Santo Domingo and returned to France, only to find it in the midst of revolution. When he arrived in Ste. Genevieve, via Philadelphia, he was penniless, according to his son. Soon, however, Guibourd became a leading citizen and married a girl from nearby Prairie du Rocher. He received a Spanish land grant in 1799 and apparently bought and lived in a nearby house until this structure was completed late in 1806. (His son's assertion that he was destitute upon arrival in town seems to offer a reasonable explanation for the long period of time it took him to build on the lot after receiving the land grant.) The house remained in the Guibourd family until 1907.

The years began taking their toll and by the 1930s, it was said to be nearing the end. Fortunately, it was purchased in 1931 by Jules Felix Valle, a wealthy St. Louis banker and a direct descendent of the last commandant. He and his wife, Anne Marie Valle—also of a prominent St. Louis family—moved there and tastefully restored the dilapidated old home during the 1930s. Mrs. Valle traveled the world—especially after her husband's death—and decorated the house with unique antiques from abroad. She died on Dec. 17, 1971, and the Foundation for Restoration of Ste. Genevieve, Inc. took control of the house after the National Trust for Historic Preservation and both of the state's historical societies turned down ownership of the house. Under the operation of the Foundation it has been open to the public as a tour house since March, 1973.

A Ghost STORY

Any town that has survived two and a half centuries is bound to have a few ghost stories. In Ste. Genevieve, the one house mentioned most frequently by long-time residents is the Guibourd-Vallé House. The historic French Colonial home has also been featured in various books of haunted Midwest abodes.

Now a popular tour house, the attractive vertical white oak log home is said to be full of things that go bump in the night.

Is the Guibourd-Vallé House haunted?

"There's no doubt in my mind," said former tour guide Carl Shinabarger. "I'm not afraid, though, because if they meant us any harm, they'd have done me in a long time ago. They're pranksters."

A columnist for the *Ste. Genevieve Herald*, Shinabarger claims to have witnessed a number of unexplainable occurrences in the old home.

"I'd hear a door open. I'd run around and look and that back door would be closed," he said. "I'd distinctly hear that door open up. There's no different sound than a door knob turning and the creak of a door opening. I'm not kidding you, one day that happened four times. I finally got aggravated and went out to the back porch and did my reading there."

While many of the creaks, knocks and other mysterious noises in the historic Guibourd-Vallé House are unexplainable, some have very concrete—and very interesting explanations. Nancy Papin Bequette and Sandy Kuehn Kertz worked as tour guides at the house in seventh and eighth grade, 1974-1976. Some 25 years after their tenure as tour guides, the two life-long friends looked back at some of the junior high pranks they perpetrated in the old house.

"A lot of the creaks and groans were us," Kertz admitted. "Zita Grannemann, who ran the house, used to tell us the ghost stories. She lived in the slave quarters and told us that there was scary stuff happening in her quarters all the time—mostly in the evenings. She would tell us the stories. We listened and then we decided to just help the stories along."

That included one girl in the attic making the dining room chandelier jingle and flicker while the other young teenage guide told of the alleged hauntings.

Something about the regally-decorated French Creole home makes those goosebump moments seem more believable. Both Bequette and Kertz admitted that they had not liked being alone in the old house and that they probably would have had little desire to work there at night.

Shinabarger relates the story of a trusted maid named Hattie who worked for Mrs. Valle for many years.

"One time Mrs. Valle came down with a bad case of something—probably pneumonia, the way it sounded," he said. "She was very, very sick, bedridden. She asked Hattie 'As a special favor, would you stay with me tonight? I want you with me.' She said 'No. I'll get the best person I can get to stay with you tonight, but I'm not staying in this house after dark.'"

The two headstones marking the graves of Mrs. Valle's dogs, Peter and Dusky, add their own element of mystery to the formal rose garden on the north side of the house.

To most visitors, though, the house feels neither spooky, nor frightening. With Anne Valle's impressive antique collection and paintings of the Valle ancestors, as well as the only original colonial casement window in the town, the Guibourd-Vallé is a warm, cozy place to visit during normal daylight hours and, on occasion, during candlelight tours—which, of course, are held after dark.

PETER
DECEMBER 3, 1950
OCTOBER 10, 19

DUSKY
SEPT. 2, 1931
JULY 20, 1946

Ste. Genevieve's Charm is Far-Reaching

Ste. Genevieve's attractive historic buildings and warm, living sense of history have inspired numerous individuals to paint, photograph, study and preserve the past.

For one little girl in the 1920s, the town held just such a magic touch. Valle Weber, great-great-great granddaughter of François Vallé II, visited the old town many times in the 1920s and '30s with her parents. She got a personally autographed copy of Father Francis Yealy's *Ste. Genevieve: The Story of Missouri's Oldest Settlement* at the city's Bicentennial in 1935. At the age of sixteen she was already hooked.

Her love and appreciation for history did not wane when she moved to Norwalk, Connecticut in 1948. In fact, it was in the historic port city that it found its calling.

Valle Weber Fay died January 22, 1998 at the age of 77, leaving behind a legacy of historic preservation and appreciation.

She became the leading force in the fight to save the historic downtown commercial district of Norwalk in the 1970s. She founded the Norwalk Preservation Trust and was one of five Norwalk preservationists to receive a U.S. Department of Interior Historic Preservation Award for "creative use of contemporary historic preservation techniques."

Like Ste. Genevieve, Norwalk has turned to those restored historic buildings as the bedrock of a thriving tourist trade.

The 1998 annual Norwalk Harbor SPLASH! Festival was dedicated to Fay's memory.

"Without Valle Fay and her cheerful, relentless determination, there would be no South Norwalk to celebrate," said the chairman of the spring celebration. "She left a legacy of elegant buildings, thriving shops, restaurants and an active water front. These are irreplaceable, unique features in the community, enjoyed by its citizens and by the many visitors who come to SoNo each year."

When Fay first began battling the wrecking ball which threatened to flatten the city's historic treasures in the 1970s, she was fighting the battle virtually alone. Yet she is remembered in the town today for her cordiality and humor.

The Vallé descendent was able to make one final visit to her ancestral home. In May, 1996 Valle and her husband, journalist Francis X. Fay, Jr. made a pilgrimage to Ste. Genevieve. It was Valle Fay's first visit here in 60 years. They were royally received by docents at both the Felix Vallé House, Mammy Shaw House and Guibourd-Vallé House. Her husband confirmed that it was her early exposure to the old homes of Ste. Genevieve that first stimulated her interest in antiquity.

Children accompanying their parents or grandparents as they stroll the streets of Ste. Genevieve should be observed with delight. Some of these youngsters may grow up to preserve a slice of heritage for future generations, just as Valle Weber Fay did.

"Les Petits Chanteurs" perform during the 25th anniversary of the Guibourd-Vallé's public life.

Autres Maisons de Haute Importance

Other Significant French Creole Vertical Log Structures

Moses Austin Outbuilding
68 S. Gabouri   c.1800
Some sources describe this as the Thomas Oliver outbuilding

Hidden behind decades—even centuries—of modifications, clapboard and layers of paint, several French Creole vertical log houses sit quietly in remote corners of the town and are not as readily visible as Ste. Genevieve's museum houses. Yet, it is the existence of these houses—along with that of their more distinguished contemporaries—that gives Ste. Genevieve its significant architectural place in history. Although the underlying vertical log structure is not always visible, the French influence can be visualized in the classic outline of the hipped roof and front porch or *galerie* of most specimens.* _–bn_

Antoine Lalumondiere
801 S. Gabouri   c.1829

Joseph Govreau
451 LeCompte c.1790-1825

Boyer Cabin
5 Boyer Place
c.1813-1826

Joseph Govreau House is listed in the HABS report of the 1980s as a heavy timber frame, but exposed members in the house (see detail photo) reveal the oldest portion of the house as a vertical log structure. An interesting feature of this house is a brick archway in the wall of the basement which appears to be the entrance to a tunnel.(Now filled in with earth.)

Thomure Cabin
873 S. Gabouri   c.1833

* *Dates based on the Historic American Buildings Survey*

Joseph
Seraphin
74 Seraphin
c.1826

François Bernier
807 Market c.1805

Beauchamp House
810 LaHaye c.1790-1805

Joseph and Louis Caron
483-499 Roberts c.1815-1825

The Joseph Caron house has an unusual construction of plank walls in two of the walls of the original house, while the end walls are timber frame. Its neighbor, the Louis Caron house, is a vertical log house.

Jean Marie Pepin dit LaChance
699 N. Fourth
c.1815-1826

LaSource-Durand Cabin *c.1807*
Moved from original site on Chadwell Lane to
Bequette-Ribault property on St. Mary Road in 1983

Charles LaHaye
704 LaPorte   c.1801

Auguste Aubuchon
467 Washington   c.1800

Limestone, Brick and Other American Ideas

The availability of limestone played a key role in building construction during the early nineteenth century. Ashlar treatment of limestone produced a gorgeous array of early nineteenth century buildings that are still aesthetically appealing today. The Louisiana Academy, the Keil-Schwent House , the Hubardeau House, the Felix Vallé Historic Site, the Dufour Stone Building, the Eloy LeCompte House and the Millard-Vallé House all made use of the eye-appealing stone. They are some of the more attractive structures in Ste. Genevieve and add considerably to the architectural importance of the town.

Keil-Schwent House c.1814

Eloy LeCompte House c.1832

Hubardeau House
c.1817 or earlier

The Louisiana Academy

Fortunately for Ste. Genevievens and lovers of architecture, two individuals, 150 years apart, came forward to save the deteriorating Louisiana Academy building. Idyllic plans, abandonment, deterioration and restoration have marked the checkered career of the grand old building.

Conceived in 1807 and chartered to provide an education for all children, boys and girls, Indian and white, the egalitarian vision that smacked of President Thomas Jefferson's enlightened philosophy was never fully put into practice due to financial restraints. The impressive ashlar stone structure was built in 1808 to house the first public school in the U.S. west of the Mississippi. Elite students from all over the Louisiana Territory came to attend the school.

Current owner Tim Conley has found the academy's original charter from 1807 and records from the school's operation, beginning in 1808. It was the first school established west of the Mississippi by the United States government—thirty to forty years before St. Louis or New Orleans had such schools. The venture had failed by 1812 and the building sat empty until 1818, when the renowned Catholic teaching order, the Christian Brothers, opened its first school in the hemisphere there in 1818. Once again children from all over the Midwest attended, with as many as thirty-four children boarding upstairs. Things fell through for the French educators as well, and the great stone building was abandoned in 1823, with the builder, Irishman William Shannon, eventually taking back title to the delinquent property.

"The deserted hill and the great white stone building which almost seemed to glow on moonlight nights, struck awe in the hearts of the supertitious slaves in the town and before long the building was considered haunted."

—Harry J. Petrequin, Stories of Old Ste. Genevieve, 1935

A circa-1850 newspaper article quotes a riverboat operator describing a "haunted house on a hill" above Ste. Genevieve. This, Conley has no doubt, was the deteriorating Louisiana Academy, then clearly visible from the Mississippi and empty for almost thirty years. Harry J. Petrequin, in his *Stories of Old Ste. Genevieve,* noted that the limestone had glowed eerily in the moonlight, adding to its haunted reputation during those years. The story of the Louisiana Academy could have ended with a late nineteenth century demolition and only a handful of surviving photographs attesting to its appearance.

Fortunately, Conley was not the first person with the vision to resurrect the building. In 1849 General Rozier entered the picture. A leading merchant, politician, historian and author, Rozier made one final attempt at starting a school in the building. Using his own immense wealth, the banker restored the abandoned structure. Soon the "Ste. Genevieve Academy" opened its doors, with Rozier as headmaster. The school, which included at least five girls, seemed to thrive and in 1853 Rozier built a large brick wing on the back of the old stone building.

After the Civil War closed the school for good, Rozier remodeled the building as a personal residence. He was allowed to assume personal ownership by the board of directors. After all, he had funneled enough of his own capital into the building to construct a whole neighborhood of residential houses in the small town.

Probably Ste. Genevieve's wealthiest citizen, Rozier decorated the house in *Empire* style, with a restrained good taste that included rosy pink walls in a daughter's bedrooms and colors such as French blue in others. The house was said to be the grandest in Ste. Genevieve County well into the early twentieth century. The general died in 1897, after writing the first published history of the town. Four of his children lived out their lives in the gradually deteriorating mansion. By 1935, the only remaining Rozier was in worse shape than the house. He went into a nursing home and the house, outbuildings and fourteen acres were sold for $8,500 to the Ste. Genevieve School District. An attractive Colonial Revival brick high school was built in 1935 next to the Old Academy. Later a modern high school and elementary school were built behind it, while the aging house served various uses and was often unoccupied. While it was restored more than once, repairs were superficial at best and deterioration began to get serious.

By the time Conley found it, a virtual wild kingdom of bats, rodents, birds and other wildlife lived in the ruin—along with legions of termites. Numerous individuals who attended the junior high (the 1935 high school building) next door during the 1970s and 1980s recall seeing a huge black wave of bats sailing into and out of the upstairs daily. Conley has just completed a painstaking four-year restoration of the grand mansion, restoring both the 1808 ashlar stone wing and the 1853 brick wing as closely as practical to their original appearances. Overby believes the symmetrical arrangements of the doors and windows give evidence of some formal architectural design—something otherwise not seen in Ste. Genevieve for nearly another century.

The front room of the Louisiana Academy decorated for the holidays.

Felix Vallé State Historic Site

The most noteworthy historically of the ashlar structures is the Felix Vallé. Now a Missouri State Historic Site, operated by the state's Department of Natural Resources, it was originally a mercantile store built by Jacob Philipson in the Federal style in 1818. It is best known as being the Menard and Vallé Mercantile, owned by Felix Vallé, son of the last commandant, Jean Baptiste Vallé. Felix Vallé was one of the leading citizens and merchants and certainly the wealthiest man in town in the late 1800s. His wife, the former Odile Pratte, became one of the old town's major characters in her own right. It was the widow Odile Vallé's benevolence that helped initiate the Valle Catholic schools and build the current parish church.

Felix Vallé lived in the house—long after the store closed—until his death in 1877. Odile lived there until her own death in 1894. During the nineteenth century the building was remodeled into a Victorian style, including a front porch. The aging Odile (affectionately known as "Mama" Vallé) was said to have stood on the porch most afternoons tossing dimes to gleeful school children returning

home from school. She also had the distinction of being the last person buried in the old Memorial Cemetery. Due to overcrowding and health concerns, further burials were banned in 1882. The widow couldn't stand the thought of not lying beside her husband and struck a deal with the city fathers. She agreed to donate a large tract of land near Valle Spring for construction of a new cemetery —if she were allowed to be interred beside her husband. Her proposal was accepted. The Valle Spring Cemetery is still in use today.

Restored to its original Federal style in the late 1970s and opened as a tourist site, the Felix Vallé is as close to its circa 1830s appearance as possible. Shelves have been placed in the store section where the outlines of the original shelves could be detected on the walls. A collection of furs and other merchandise used in the trade-based economy of the time is on display. The East room is a parlor, like it

was during the Vallé's lifetime. Upstairs, the couple's bedroom is authentically restored, including a huge *armoire*. Recent renovations have removed the modern office space of the DNR out of the building and across the street to the Mammy Shaw House. The outbuilding directly behind the Vallé House is also unique. It is one of the few surviving early nineteenth century outbuildings in town.

Storytelling at the Felix Vallé State Historic Site

RECONSTRUCTING
Ste. Genevieve

Thanks to the talents of Ste. Genevieve scale-modeler Lewis Pruneau, visitors and locals alike no longer need to rely on their imaginations to try and envision what the streets of Ste. Genevieve were like in the early 19th Century.

Pruneau, a winner of several national awards for his World War II dioramas, has built a 1:225 scale model of the town as it might have appeared around 1830. The piece captures the town when it was still a French village, but with some early Anglo-American influences already visible. A particularly interesting element of the diorama is the Ste. Genevieve Catholic Rock Church which is depicted under construction.

Research for the project was conducted by Site Administrator Jim Baker and Bill Miller of the Felix Vallé State Historic Site. Relying heavily on Brown's 1840 survey conducted for the U.S. government plus hands-on investigation of Ste. Genevieve's remaining Creole and Anglo-American structures, they prepared detailed drawings from which Pruneau worked.

The 9x11 foot diorama features well over 100 houses and outbuildings and is housed in the Amoureux House. The project was funded by *Les Amis*, a support group interested in preserving the French heritage of the area.

Mammy Shaw House

Sharing the Merchant and Second Street corner with the Dufour and the Felix Vallé is the Mammy Shaw House, named for the widow Emilie "Mammy" Shaw, who lived alone in the house from her husband's death in 1849 until her own in 1897. Her husband, Dr. Benjamin Shaw, bought the original two-room heavy timber frame house (built in 1818) from Jean Baptiste Bossier and added the back room and the upstairs area. He is also believed to have built the unique stone kitchen behind the house. During the past thirty years the historic buildings were connected by a stone studio constructed in the 1960s by local artist Matt Ziegler. Two of his works are displayed in the Shaw House.

Like the Felix Vallé, the Shaw House gives up its secrets through original paint on the walls. The locations of Bossier's 1818 shelves and counters can be easily seen. The house also

The Stone Kitchen behind the Shaw House

boasts some interesting hardware and a most unusual group of doors. Somehow the widow reportedly obtained the glass doors from the steamboat *Dr. Franklin II* after its tragic explosion in 1852. The original panes of the doors are etched and cut glass.

Millard-Vallé House

Another notable double pile structure is the Millard-Vallé House, an impressive ashlar stone on North Main between the northern city limits and Little Rock Landing. Records show that the property was purchased by a Josiah Millard in 1810 and eventually sold at a substantially higher price to Jean Baptiste Vallé in 1828 for his son François Vallé and his wife Catherine "Zouzou" Beauvais Vallé. The price would seem to suggest that a house had been built under Millard's ownership, however, dendrochronology dates the house c.1834. Owners believe this could be due to extensive work done to the house at that time. The grand house, with its ten fireplaces and hand-sanded pine floors, has been thoroughly restored by its owners, Frank and Shirley Myers and children as their private residence. The house, which has been featured in national magazines on country living and historic preservation, narrowly escaped ruin in the 1993 and '95 floods.

The Dufour Stone Building(1818) is another remarkable commercial building that has survived nearly two centuries of constant commercial use. With its original structural system virtually intact, the structure is one of the many unsung gems in the rich architectural tapestry of Ste. Genevieve. It was at one time owned by Dr. Lewis F. Linn, an early U.S. Senator from Missouri. Serving as

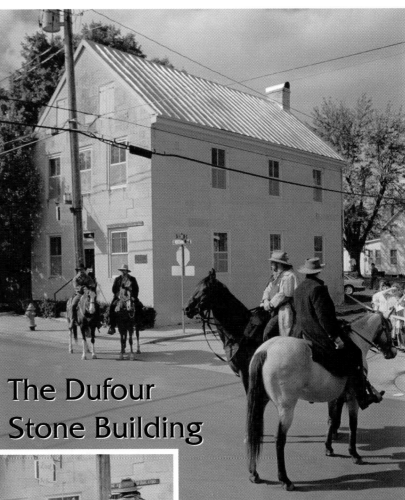

The Dufour Stone Building

A mock bank robbery staged during Ste. Genevieve's Fall Festival at the old Rozier Bank Building.

the Henry L. Rozier Bank from 1891 until 1964, it was the site of a daring bank robbery on November 1, 1939. City Marshal Henry J. Drury was shot in a gun battle after catching up with the robbers six miles out of town. The marshal survived and the three robbers, who took $2,200, were each caught and sentenced to fifteen years in prison. The South and East corners of the building are of dressed, or ashlar stone otherwise unseen in Ste. Genevieve at the time, while the sides not facing the street are of field stone. In this, it is similar to the later Millard-Vallé House.

Southern Hotel

As the first decade of the 1800s slipped past, the Americans were making their presence felt more and more. Not only were ashlar stone buildings becoming popular with the affluent, the American double-pile brick building was also beginning to catch on.

The grand old Southern Hotel is another of the truly awe-inspiring sights for a first-time visitor. The greatest portion of the house was built by John Donohue circa 1820. This double pile brick was extensively enlarged and remodeled during the Greek Revival period and afterward. The bracketed eaves, belvedere, dormers and octagonal newel at the first floor landing seem to come from the 1870s or 1880s. Like the Louisiana Academy, it appears to have been built with a central hallway, making Overby think it had some formal architectural design.

In the late 1800s, lookouts would watch for riverboats from the "granny's cooler" atop the building and send horse-drawn "buses" to pick up the passengers. The Southern Hotel, authentically restored and operated by Mike and Barbara Hankins as a bed and breakfast, has been featured in national magazines and on public television.

Price Old Brick House

Although historians no longer consider it the first brick building built west of the Mississippi, the Price Old Brick House at the corner of Market and Third is no doubt among the oldest surviving ones west of the river and maintains much of its original exterior appearance. Built around 1804, the Old Brick House was certainly the first brick building in Ste. Genevieve. It has served as a territorial court house, a school, a residence and—for the past half-century—a popular saloon and restaurant.

Ratte-Hoffman House

Located on a commanding precipice above the South Gabouri Creek, the old ruin, known by such various names as the Ratte-Hoffman House, the LaBruyere House, the Ratte-LaBruyere House and the John McArthur House, is likely too far gone to be saved. What a spectacular sight it makes, though, as the grand circa-1809 Federal I-house gallantly fights for its life. Before the floods of the 1990s the rusting cars of various eras encircled the old house, creating a true artistic creation. During the author's first adult visit to the old town in 1986, it was the Ratte-Hoffman and its equally deteriorating antique car bodies that captured his attention more than the restored homes. He circled the property several times, enthralled. To many, the dilapidated early nineteenth century house and the rusting twentieth century vehicles present a poetic slice of Americana.

If the Ratte-Hoffman cannot be saved, it is a pity. One of the earliest examples of the in-coming American influence, the heavy-timber frame I-house maintains much of its original appearance—including most likely its original interior plan. A large two-story back porch—slowly pulling away from the house—was a distinctive feature. Overby suggests that "it may be the best preserved American frame house built (in Ste. Genevieve) in the first decade of the nineteenth century." The shuttered door on the second floor suggests a center hallway, like the Louisiana Academy, built about the same time.

With the projected urban design levee's south closure running close behind the property, the cars may by necessity be removed from the site. Let us hope the grand old house, if not saved, can at least be allowed to die naturally. It is not only a spectacular find for photographers and artists, it also reminds one of what all the eighteenth and early nineteenth century buildings might look like if preservationists had not stepped in during the past few decades.

Moses Austin Cabin

Moses Austin, a Connecticut Yankee who followed the scent of lead to the region, became the future state's first true industrialist. A lead miner in New England and Virginia, he was lured to Spanish Louisiana by tales of the richness of lead veins.

Austin and his family lived in Ste. Genevieve from September, 1798 until his palatial "Durham Hall" was completed in Mine Au Breton (now Potosi) in June, 1799. Austin continued to own land and buildings in Ste. Genevieve, although whether he owned a large mansion on the grounds where the Moses Austin Outbuilding now stands is questionable.

While in Ste. Genevieve, the Yankee—with the aide of Welch lawyer John Rice Jones of Kaskaskia—formed a partnership with Commandants François Vallé II and Pierre DeLassus DeLuziere and got the two men's aid in getting a land grant at Mine Au Breton.

Austin brought modern lead smelting practices to the region for the first time and revolutionized the trade. Worth some $200,000 at the outbreak of the War of 1812, Austin suffered financial reversals thereafter and was briefly imprisoned for debts. Late in life he became obsessed with the dream of getting a land grand in the untapped Spanish region now comprising Texas. He died in 1821, before the dream was realized, but his son Stephen F. Austin would lead the original 300 settlers from Potosi to Texas and earn immortality even greater than that of his ambitious father.

The house, which stands on the Moses Austin property and is now believed to be one of his outbuildings, is of Anglo-American brick-nogged heavy-timber frame construction and dated circa 1810 with later 19th Century additions. In 1840 the building ownership passed to a free woman of color who had formerly been Austin's slave. The house and property were purchased in 1987 by the Jour de Fête Committee which maintains the building and uses the property for its annual arts and crafts fair.

Anglo-American Vernacular Heavy Timber Frame

The American influence of the early 19th Century made itself felt in the architecture of the period. Characterized by their heavily timbered framing, a number of structures remain standing from that era. Except where noted, most of the specimens here are of the vertical timber style with or without brick or stone nogging between the uprights. *—bn*

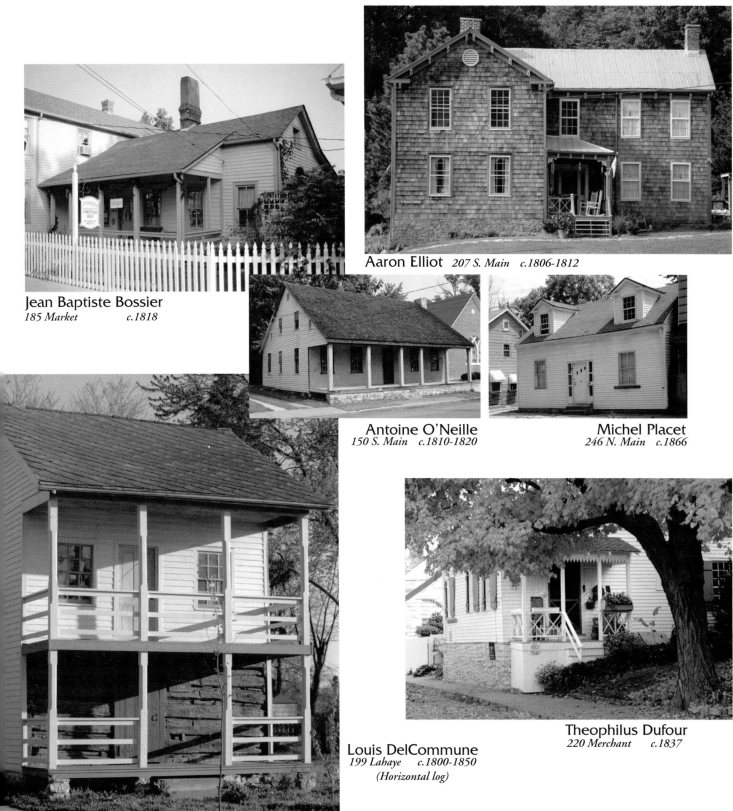

Aaron Elliot *207 S. Main   c.1806-1812*

Jean Baptiste Bossier
185 Market   c.1818

Antoine O'Neille
150 S. Main   c.1810-1820

Michel Placet
246 N. Main   c.1866

Theophilus Dufour
220 Merchant   c.1837

Louis DelCommune
199 Lahaye   c.1800-1850
(Horizontal log)

Dr. Walter Fenwick *Fifth and Merchant   c.1850*

Abraham Newfield-Sen. Lewis Linn *223 Merchant   c.1806*

François Bernier *(Horizontal log)*
43 S. Eighth   c.1838

Etienne Govreau *415 Lahaye   c.1800-1840*

Augustine Aubuchon Jr.
Fourth and Roberts   c.1815-1826

Galleria Frame Shop
46 S. Main   c.1850

François Morel Aubuchon
53 Washington   c.1806-1848

Sebastian Butcher
229 S. Gabouri   c.1818

Marie LaPorte
248 Market   c.1830

Achtung!
The German Brick Era Arrives

Today the influence of the nineteenth century Germans in Ste. Genevieve is perhaps more evident than that of the pioneer French. Beginning in the 1840s, the town and much of the county were fairly inundated with the fastidious German immigrants. With them came not only a propensity for neatness and hard work, but a skill for building with brick.

The German vernacular brick buildings began to spring up shortly before 1850 and dominated the rest of the nineteenth century landscape. Most of these impressive houses and commercial structures are still standing and in daily use.

One of the earlier ones is the Firmin A. Rozier Store. Built about 1850, the brick building was where Rozier practiced law early in his career. Overby speculates that Rozier hired a German bricklayer. He points out its similarity to the Pierre Schumert House and the John Hael House.

Pierre Schumert *73 N. Main c.1849-1851*

John Hael *159 N. Main   c.1860*

Firmin Rozier
124 Merchant   c.1850

Andere Deutchen Beispiele
Other German Examples

Martin Intress *52 N. Third c.1842-1846*

Leucke/Obermiller *341 /351 N. Main c.1865/c.1850*

Oberle House *176 N. Main c.1865*

Steigerhaus *1021 Market c.1890*

Charles Jokerst *737 N. Fourth c.1850*

Augustus Gisi *Market and Hwy. 61 c.1860*

Hettig-Naumann *299 Seraphin c.1858*

Holy Cross Lutheran Church

The Romanesque-style Holy Cross Lutheran Church on Second and Market—originally named "The German Lutheran Evangelical Church"—appears today much as it did when it was erected between 1869-1875 with the exception of the adjoining education building which was added in 1990.

The influx of Germans in the 1840s to the Ste. Genevieve area brought mostly German Catholics. Unlike the Saxon Lutherans who settled as a group in the Perry County region, the German Lutherans who arrived in Ste. Genevieve in the 1860s were comprised of individuals and families. Because of its small congregation size throughout most of its history, it was predominantly served by itinerant pastors until 1929.

Its first pastor, the Reverend Otto F. Voigt, was installed in 1869 and opened a school in the church. Previously, most of the children had been attending the Roman Catholic

Children of the Holy Cross Lutheran Church ride in a float in the 1985 250th Parade depicting the early German School

School. When Voigt left Ste. Genevieve to pastor in Friedenburg, Missouri in 1871, Johann Siegmund L. Deffner, an ordinary, filled in for itinerant pastors, organized a choir named *Liederkranz*, and taught the school's lessons in both German and English. The school was known as the German School and was served by Deffner until 1890 when he resigned because of illness.

In 1929 when the church finally had a resident pastor, Rev. Ernest A. Brockmann, the church's enthusiasm was rekindled, and electric lights, a new stove and hymnals were added. With each succeeding pastor, improvements were made to the interior including the digging of a basement with pick and shovel beneath the church in 1942.

It was in 1983 that the church saw revival again with the advent of Rev. Richard Thur as pastor. A new education building was added in 1990 and today with Bible studies, youth groups, a jail ministry and signing of the worship service for the deaf, the congregation has finally seen such growth that a second Sunday worship service has been added. *–psn*

18–Ev. Luth.–69 Kreuz Kirche

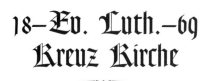

With the inscription above the door, the Lutheran Church is the oldest standing church structure in town.

Town Square

As we continue our architectural stroll beneath the glow of Ste. Genevieve's street lamps, we note a few more of her significant façades. From the pre-Civil War commercial structures to the Eastlake and Italianate ornamentation of the commercial buildings popular in the post-Civil War era, even to the modern adaptation of the new courthouse wing—all dominated by the towering Gothic presence of the Catholic Church steeple—the town square represents a slice of the myriad styles so conducive to Ste. Genevieve's charm.

Third St. on the Square with the Anvil Restaurant (c.1870) in foreground.

The Old Rock Church

Ste. Genevieve Catholic Church

"We shall not understand the character of these French pioneers, unless we appreciate the profound effect which religion had on their lives," wrote Father Francis J. Yealy in his 1935 *Ste. Genevieve: The Story of Missouri's Oldest Settlement.*

Inversely, Carl Ekberg writes in his book *Colonial Ste. Genevieve,* "The Roman Catholism in colonial Ste. Genevieve was earthy and robust...rooted in the rhythms of life in an agricultural community."

Whether it was their religion that gave character to the French pioneers, or the French pioneers who gave character to their religion, the founding of Ste. Genevieve was well rooted in Catholism. The story begins with the missionary Jesuits who risked their lives crossing the dangerous Mississippi from their mother Church of the Immaculate Conception in Kaskaskia (1750-1774) in order to administer the sacraments to the parish of St. Joachim (later to be known as Ste. Genevieve). Their subsequent expulsion by the French government in France and all French colonies(1763-64) was an unexpected blow to the French colonists. From the unstable Capuchin Friar Hilaire(1773-77), to the beloved but much afflicted Father Gibault, the church's history itself is colorful indeed.

It was through the influence of German Carmelite Rev. Paul von Heiligenstein, a.k.a. St. Pierre, and François Vallé II that the exodus to higher ground took place and the log church was reconstructed from the old timbers at its new site in 1795. Three priests—St. Pierre; Irish priest Fr. James Maxwell, who died after being thrown from his horse; and Fr. Henri Pratte, the first native-born priest west of the Mississippi who was responsible for improvements which maintained the structure for another 20 years—served in the log church at the site. Both Pratte and Maxwell are interred beneath the church. It was replaced by a stone church erected about 1831 by Vincentian Rev. Francis X. Dahmen. Due to the influx of German and English speaking people to the area and the difficulty of hearing confessions in different tongues, Dahmen undertook the task of beginning a new school.

Odile Delassus Pratte Vallé, twice-widowed, had joined the Sisters of Loretto. By 1837, she financed the school by purchasing the Catherine Bolduc house (the present day Bolduc-LeMeilleur) and the brick store adjoining it.

"Let us add to it a steeple that will tower and rise toward heaven, and a cross upon its summit that will overlook everything also made by the hands of man of our town, and shine with approbation to the surrounding country."

—Ste. Genevieve Fair Play, May 1874

The Sisters of Loretto stayed and taught until 1849 when they moved their school to the "rock house" slave quarters on the Joseph Pratte property opposite the church. In 1858, the sisters left town and Father J. M. St. Cyr brought in the Sisters of St. Joseph to Ste. Genevieve. They served the Catholic schools as educators for over 120 years. In 1893, a three-story building was erected for the school and remained in use until 1954.

Rev. Francis Xavier Weiss built the stone building next to the rock church in 1865 with the intentions of a college to be taught by the Christian Brothers. When not able to procure the Brothers as teachers, he abandoned the idea and moved into the building himself, tearing down the dilapidated rectory.

On May 28, 1874 this abridged editorial appeared in the Ste. Genevieve Fair Play:

"We would call the attention of the directors of the church, and the people in general, that our Catholic Church is too small for our congregational community, which is clearly visible to us all. We, therefore, believe it to be high time for us to think of undertaking this great and noble work which should have been done years ago. The church door is at all times crowded with persons during the holy sacrifice of the Mass who cannot procure for themselves a seat, being also a great drawback to many others who are compelled to stand up during the hours of divine service, which is a great inducement for them to leave during sermons, causing much disturbance to our pastor and congregation; the majority of who, we are convinced, would remain if comfortably seated, … Gentlemen directors, we have a very inconvenient, narrow, and winding stairway, hardly admissible for the passage of one person; the same being in a very dilapidated condition, the walls and floor of which are literally covered with tobacco juice and for years back have been invariably neglected. This should not be tolerated in the church of our divine Master and God."

Apparently, the editorial made an impression, because in the spring of 1876 work began on the construction of the present Gothic revival structure. Services continued in the old rock church as the new brick structure was built around and over it. The rock church was eventually dismantled and carried out the doors. The foundation of the rock church is visible in the basement of the present church. The church was dedicated in 1880 at a total cost of $24,000.

Following Fr. Weiss' death in 1901, the Rev. Charles L. van Tourenhout was appointed pastor.

In 1911, seeing the need for more seating, Fr. Van remodeled the church. The removal of the west wall and the erection of a hexagonal apse and two small transepts were just a few of the many changes. Interestingly, in designing the additions, Fr. Van had made provisions for his own burial under the church, but was denied the privilege. He loved ritual and revived the Corpus Christi procession through town, midnight mass at Christmas, and the singing of French hymns. Fr. Van was also responsible for founding Valle High School in 1925, building a new rectory, and turning the former stone rectory into the high school.

Structurally the church remains relatively unaltered from its 1911 remodeling. It stands as a place of reverence, awe, solitude and sanctuary. –psn

Concelebrating the Eucharist with Archbishop Justin Rigali.

The sanctuary of Ste. Genevieve Catholic Church regally decorated for Christmas.

Bogy-Bussen House

The grand Italianate Bogy House (circa 1810 with 1870 additions) at 163 Merchant was home not only to the native-born lawyer and senator Lewis V. Bogy, but also to Alvin Charles and Margery Boverie Bussen, two of Ste. Genevieve's great benefactors. Founder and owner of Bussen's Quarry, later bought by Tower Rock, the Bussens were quiet, unpretentious people who dedicated much of their estate towards the betterment of Ste. Genevieve, the Catholic Church and Valle Schools. In 1953, they donated a large tract of land for the establishment of Ste. Genevieve's Père Marquette Park, a beautiful stretch of land which overlooks the Mississippi River near Little Rock landing. The park is home to the Valle, Ste. Gen. and Yanks baseball teams as well as the city and Valle soccer leagues. The municipal swimming pool is located there as are the city tennis courts.

After her husband's death in 1978, Mrs. Bussen's generosity continued when she donated the Boverie building, which had housed her family's general store on the square, to the Ste. Genevieve Parish. Margery extended her hospitality even to the weary Jour de Fête visitor, who, in needing a place to sit or a drink of cold water, was invited onto her front porch.

"The Bussens were very generous people," said one couple who knew them well. "They were unassuming people. You didn't know they were wealthy by looking at them. Margery did not spend it on herself, she spent it on others."

After her death on Valentine's Day 1990, Ste. Genevieve found that it had received a huge valentine from Mrs. Bussen—a $3 million endowment to offset the operational costs of a proposed community center. Of the possible sites considered for the center, one was the Père Marquette Park which the Bussens had made possible four decades earlier. But in the interest of county expansion and industrial growth, the powers-that-be determined upon a location outside the city limits on Hwy 32.

In 1999, the house was converted from a private residence to be used as a fine eclectic dining establishment. *–psn, mle*

Judge Peter Huck House

The 1906 Judge Peter Huck house (now home to Elmer and Betty Donze) at the southwest corner of Fourth and Merchant Streets is considered the finest of the late Queen Anne homes in town and is one of the handful of twentieth century limestone structures in Ste. Genevieve. Although it took the place of an extremely historic circa-1800 French Creole house built by Charles Gregoire, it contributes handsomely to the historic downtown itself.

Charles Gregoire was a major figure in turn-of-the-nineteenth century Ste. Genevieve. His vertical log home appeared to be similar to its next door neighbor, the Guibourd-Vallé and other Creole houses.

Decades before the idea of historic preservation entered the most conscientious of minds, the old colonial home was demolished to give Peter Huck–state legislator, circuit judge and prosecuting attorney during a long and distinguished career–the finest home in town.

The Gregoire family later constructed the fine Greek Revival mansion at 51 South Fourth around 1850. This brick side-passage town house is the only one of its kind in Ste. Genevieve.

The Gregoire House

Jules Petrequin-Knights of Columbus House

Jules Petrequin built his impressive mansion at 600 Market Street in 1912. His son Frederick showed his excitement over his new home when he sent a postcard of the house to Anna Vorst (later Thomure) who was attending the State Normal School in Cape Girardeau at the time. "Well, here's our new house," he wrote.

Jules Petrequin was a part owner of Western Lime Works where he served as general manager. He was also a director and large stockholder in the Home Light and Water Company.

Viola Oberle worked for the Petrequins nursing their crippled son Nicholas for whom it was said the mansion was built. She was later assisted by her husband, Fred, who maintained the house and grounds. When Jules died, the Oberles were invited to move into the residence which they eventually did. The house came into the possession of the couple upon Mrs. Petrequin's death in 1950.

The Knights of Columbus purchased the home from the Oberles in 1959 to be used as their meeting hall. The Fair Play headline proclaimed, "Knights Have a Castle." With its massive columns, rounded porch, terraced lawn and expansive grounds, it is indeed a majestic sight. A wing was added in the '70s offering the community an elegant location for anniversary and wedding receptions._bn

The 1962 Knights of Columbus Choir with director Doris Hipes.

Will Brooks House

Although not grand, but of equal importance to the cultural heritage of Ste. Genevieve, the surviving late 19th century African-American vernacular homes on St. Mary Road near Seraphin have stories of their own to be told, and are therefore worthy of preservation. Both are double pen I-houses built between 1850 and 1880 and are typical of African-American construction of the period. One is currently well-maintained and occupied. Its neighbor at 311 St. Mary Road sits deteriorating with Virginia creeper climbing up the siding and through the windows. It was here that William Brooks, a respected black gentleman and World War I veteran, raised his highly successful sons. The area was known as "mudtown," traditionally a mixed neighborhood where black and white children played together.

Born in Ste.Genevieve in 1889, Will Brooks worked in the service of historian Captain Gustavus St. Gem and banker Henry L. Rozier (both Sr. and Jr.) in what is now the Felix Vallé House, and later for Anne Valle. He married Johannah McNabb on July 14, 1928. She was a Lincoln University graduate and Ste. Genevieve's first resident African-American with a college degree. She taught at the Lincoln School (now First School Day Care) and in 1941 became a professor at Stowe Teachers College (now Harris-Stowe University) in St. Louis. Tragically, her blossoming life was cut

Two examples of African-American double pen I-houses sit on St. Mary Road. The Will Brooks home is in foreground.

short. She was killed in a car wreck at age 37 in 1942. Will Brooks was left to bring up three young sons on his own.

While working for the Roziers and later for Anne Valle, he had unlimited access to the family vehicles. According to his youngest son Jack, Will would check on the young boys several times a day during the summer to make sure they were staying out of mischief. Will and Johannah Brooks' spotless reputation helped keep their family's life placid, despite occasional turbulence around them,(See story, p. 36).

The Brooks' oldest two sons had to catch a Greyhound bus every morning for high schools in Festus and St. Louis. It wasn't until Jack's senior year (1954-55) that Brown vs. the Topeka Board of Education opened the doors for blacks to enter previously all-white schools.

Jack enrolled in Valle High School and immediately made the Warrior football team. Valle had trouble procuring his transcripts from Douglass School in Crystal City where he had attended his first three years of high school, so he transferred to Ste. Genevieve

The Lincoln School, c.1859 (now First School Day Care) at 145 Washington—Harvey/Wilson restoration

High School. He recalled playing football against Perryville on a Sunday afternoon for Valle and again the next Friday night in a Ste. Genevieve Dragons uniform.

"Jack was probably one of the most popular kids in class," said Lorraine Stange, a fellow 1955 SGHS graduate and a childhood playmate of the Brooks children. "He was well-liked. His family had always been well-respected."

That respect was manifested in recent years when the city named a street "Brooks Drive" in Will Brooks' honor. A special display on the Brooks family has also been set up at the Felix Vallé House in past years as part of Black History Month.

"Will Brooks was kind and unassuming," said Stange. "He was the type of person who lived his Christianity."

"To me, Bill Brooks was the last gentleman in Ste. Genevieve," commented Teresa Drury, a longtime resident of Ste. Genevieve. "He was the last man to tip his hat to women. The men all used to do that, but he was the last one."

The Birke Houses

John Birke (or Burk), was a blacksmith from Germany who came to Ste. Genvieve around 1795. He had bought a mulatto slave woman, originally from Virginia, named Rachel Prior. After having two children by her, Jean Baptiste and Mary Ann, Birke freed Rachel and the two were married in August of 1801 by Fr. James Maxwell. Birke's stone house on Third Street and the vertical log house once owned by his son on Ziegler are significant for their architecture and for their mulatto traditions.

Jean Baptiste Birke   *151 Ziegler   c.1800-1845*

The Jean Baptiste Birke house was one of four structures purchased with revolving funds by the Missouri Department of Natural Resources following the flood of 1993. Those houses, listed in the National Register of Historic Places, were deemed important enough to be preserved rather than demolished in the flood buy-out program. They await a suitable purchaser interested in undertaking the important work of preservation.

John Birke Stone House   *398 N. Third   c.1812*

PRESERVING
THE PAST
FOR THE FUTURE

Funding for this project provided by:
Missouri Department of Natural Resources
Historic Preservation Revolving Fund
P.O. Box 176, Jefferson City, MO 65102
1-800-334-6946

An Architectural Sampler

A Look at Some of Ste. Genevieve's Other Architectural Treasures

299 Academy   Tudor, 1935

*199 Merchant   **Jesse B. Robbins House**   Italianate, c.1867*

375 Seraphin   Builder's Queen Anne, c.1900

171 S. Second   T-plan, c.1894-1901

246 Jefferson   Builder's Queen Anne, c.1900

*67 N. Fourth   **J.B. Roberts**   Builder's Queen Anne, c.1893-1908*

Etienne Parent
Restored by Robert and Odile Mecker
102 S. Main, Commercial, c.1809-1844
"Colonial Thymes" Coffee Shop

199 N. Fourth   *Italianate, c.1880*

64 N. Second   *Greek Revival, c.1850*
Augustus Bequette

1 Chadwell Lane   *Greek Revival, c.1850*
Chadwell-Leavenworth

301 S. Gabouri   *Builder's Queen Anne, c.1911*
Thomure House

698 N. Third   *Builder's Queen Anne, c.1900*

406 N. Third   *Builder's Queen Anne, c.1900*

Fourth and Jefferson   *Italianate, c.1887*
Leon Yealy   *Birthplace of historian Rev. F.J. Yealy, S.J.*

98 N. Third   *Four Square, 1931*

Valentine Rottler   *501 N. Third, Central I-House, c.1876*

198 N. Main   *Commercial Frame, c.1870*
Henry Wilder

A Brewing Tradition

Even the Richardsonian Romanesque tradition is represented in the fine old, albeit dilapidated, Ste. Genevieve Brewery, c.1895. Although, it is not for its architectural style that the Ste. Genevieve Brewing and Lighting Company is remembered. Located at 555 North Third in the area of town once known as "coopertown" after the barrel cooperage in which the golden elixer was stored, the Ste. Genevieve Brewery was actively fermenting its malts during the early part of the 20th century. The 1908 Drummers Convention catalog had this to say about the brewery—"The products of this brewery are widely known for their purity and excellent qualities. Associated with the nectar of the gods, and in fact, manufac-

tured therefrom, is the claim of the Ste. Genevieve Brewing and Lighting Association for the product which they have been offering to the public for the past fourteen years, and perhaps at few points in the United States, have brewers found a more agreeable spot in which to practice their alchemistry which has so delightful a result for millions of people, i.e. lager beer. The careful attention given to the proper fermentation and aging are responsible for the high estimation with which the Ste. Genevieve beers are regarded by the public at large. *Success* is the name of the brewery's popular bottled beer and *Special Pale* their draught beer."_bn_

Second Empire

In the middle of the German and commercial landscape on North Main, sit three fine examples of Second Empire construction with their heavy post-Civil War Victorian ornamentation.

Main Street Inn

The attractive 1882 Main Street Inn, (formerly the Meyer Hotel), at 221 N. Main was handsomely restored in the 1990s by Ken and Karen Kulberg and operates today as one of Ste. Genevieve's fine bed and breakfast establishments.

Charles Hertich House

In the Hertich House (c. 1850) at 99 N. Main, home of noted nineteenth century physician Charles A. Hertich, the basement gives evidence of a circa-1810 structure having existed there prior to the building of this house. The house, since 1999, has served as an annex to the Inn St. Gemme Beauvais.

Bertha Doerge House

The Bertha Doerge House, c.1880, at 222 N. Main, was home to the beloved midwife who was said to have delivered more babies in Ste. Genevieve County than any one doctor ever did.

The Cone Mill exploded July 16, 1880 in what the *Ste. Genevieve Fair Play* called "the greatest calamity that has ever befallen our city." Two men were killed and one severely burned as the flour mill's two steam boilers blew. Superintendent Martin Meyer was one of the fatalities, hit in the head by debris. His widow, Mary Meyer Baumstark, was said to have used his life insurance money in 1882 to build the Meyer Hotel (now Main Street Inn) next to the Elroy LeCompte House (which served as an annex to the hotel for several years).

Seemingly jinxed, the Cone Mill was among the numerous structures hit hard on June 19, 1897 when a fierce windstorm hit the town. Called a tornado by the *Fair Play* and a cyclone by the *Herald*, the storm blew off part of the roof, the cupola, and both smokestacks.

The building housed the MFA Mill and Feed Store in the mid-1900s and today is home to The Mill/Antique Mart.

Inn St. Gemme Beauvais/Felix Rozier House

Brothers Felix and Francis Rozier each built stately brick mansions on adjoining lots on

North Main around 1848. The influential brothers were leading businessmen throughout the nineteenth century.

Dr. Osmund Overby of the University of Missouri believes the Felix Rozier House (now the Inn St. Gemme Beauvais at 78 North Main) originally consisted of just the southern half of the present building. Built during the Greek Revival period, he feels it may have been a side passage house similar to the Gregoire House on South Fourth.

The Felix Rozier House had the good fortune to pass into the Donze family. Lawrence Donze bought it in 1923. Twenty-five years later he passed the house on to his son, Norbert Donze who, along with his wife Frankye, would go on to become probably the most significant local historic restorers in Ste. Genevieve. They converted the stately house into an inn before it left the family. It continues to operate today as one of Ste. Genevieve's highly reputable B and Bs.

Francis Rozier House

Mary Rozier Sharp recalled growing up in the Francis Rozier House in her Rozier family biography, *Between the Gabouri,* which she authored with her husband, Louis J. Sharp, III.

"We used most of the eighteen rooms all the time and all of them some of the time," she wrote. "It was a home for cousins' visits, slumber parties, weekends from boarding school, balls, weddings and funerals."

She recalled a vegetable garden behind the house, outlined by boxwood shrubs. A blackberry patch and fruit trees sat further back from the house. An attractive wrought iron fence on a stone foundation lined the Main Street side of the property, while Sharp recalled a green wooden fence facing Merchant Street.

The Francis Rozier mansion was not so lucky as its neighboring counterpart. It became one of the last victims of pre-tourism insensitivity to historic architecture. Although the grand old house was still sturdy and attractive, it was deemed less important than downtown parking space. Although space could have been

made across the street, before the 1949 construction of the First Baptist Church, or opposite the Felix Rozier, where a car wash would go, the Rozier lot became the virginal sacrifice to progress. The great brick home was torn down in the summer of 1957. The steps from the sidewalk to the front door are still visible on the edge of the parking lot. This was one move many residents wish could be taken back.

A break in the rock wall at the crosswalk on Main Street marks the location of the gate of the Francis Rozier House.

127

A Preservation Success Story
The Kempff-Jaccard Buildings

One of the most dramatic sagas of impending demolition in Ste. Genevieve came in 1983, when the historic Kempff-Jaccard Buildings appeared to be ready to meet the headache ball on several different occasions.

Built in 1851, the large brick Kempff Building (more commonly known as the Stanton Building) was the oldest commercial building on Market Street, east of the courthouse square. It's stately stepped gables gave evidence

that it had been built in two parts. The adjoining Jaccard Building, built about 1860, was smaller, but equally charming.

Both had interesting histories. The Jaccard Building was built by jeweler P.U. Jaccard and housed his first jewelry store. He later transferred his business to St. Louis, where the Jaccard Jewelers continue to flourish.

The Stanton Building enjoyed its greatest claim to fame in the twentieth century. It was here, in 1912, that Edward Stanton opened one of the first car dealerships and garages in town. According to a 1949 Fair Play article, Stanton sold his first car to railroad mogul John Tlapek of St. Mary. Stanton was officially granted a Ford franchise dealership December 22, 1912—one of the first in Missouri. Stanton, of course, broke in during the heyday of the Model T. That first year there were just four cars in town. Stanton had to buy three cars, deposit a specified amount of money and buy some $300 worth of parts to get the franchise.

The building later served as the public library when it outgrew its corner of the Museum. By the beginning of the 1980s, it had stood empty and decrepit for a number of years. Ste. Genevieve County purchased the building in 1981 with the expressed purpose of demolishing it to create more parking spaces.

The drama began in the late summer of 1983. In August, the county commission requested a demolition permit from the city. Much to the commissioners' dismay, the front page story in the August 17 Herald stating that the building was doomed, created a whirl of opposition. The community had changed in the past twenty-five years. More local citizens realized the value of the city's unique architectural heritage. The love of historic buildings fostered by Lucille Basler and others had taken root. The Landmarks Commission immediately urged the county to wait until a University of Missouri historical architecture survey team could determine its possible historic significance and restoration potential.

Letters began appearing in the Herald, urging the Commission to keep the old buildings. Arguments were made that the loss of any more historic structures could hurt tourism and that it was "economic folly" to pay for demolition and gain only half a dozen parking spaces. "Steady erosion of the beauty of this town will just as steadily erode the tourist dollar as well," one letter-writer predicted.

With opposition to the demolitions rising quickly, the board of aldermen voted unanimously to reject a demolition permit. To their surprise, however, the commission cited an opinion from the county prosecuting attorney that it did not need the city's permission. The buildings would be torn down regardless.

A public hearing was set to discuss the matter. The noted architectural historian, Dr. Osmund Overby, meanwhile, checked out the building and stated that the study "has clearly identified these buildings as important to the historic and architectural character of the community, as ones that should be preserved." He noted that "Enough has already been lost in this block, so that if these buildings should go as well, that historic character of the block would be dealt a major loss right in the heart of Ste. Genevieve."

Patrick H. Steele, executive vice president of the Missouri Heritage Trust agreed. "The proposal to demolish these buildings on a major street in the center of a National Landmark District represents the loss of significant buildings, a loss that will be felt not only in Ste. Genevieve, but by all who visit there."

The commission agreed to postpone the demolition so that a six-person committee could study alternatives. This committee consisted of Pat Schwent, Stan Drury, Janey Scott, Jerry Fallert, Phil Vawter and Steele with Presiding Commissioner Adrian Ehler acting as chairman. The committee was given forty-five days to find a buyer who would pay $50,000 for the property. If not, the county road and bridge crew would begin demolition on November 1.

Jack F. Rasmussen, chief of the Corps of Engineers' St. Louis district planning division supported the earlier concerns that demolition could hurt the chances of a levee. In mid-October he noted that "the issue of protection of these and other historic buildings does have a bearing on flood protection for the community" and that the case had "given the corps the opportunity to observe how the existing local controls operate and how important historic structures are to the local community."

At the end of October, the committee came back with a recommendation that the county hang onto and rent the buildings or try to sell them for fair value. In early November, the county commission decided to reapply for a demolition permit anyway—although the commissioners were still willing to talk to any would-be buyers. In a November 16 editorial entitled "Time to Put Up," Herald publisher

Ralph Morris challenged an individual or company to come forward and noted that the only additional provision he would like to see would require the buyer "to guarantee their proper preservation as a part of the historic heritage of our community."

Christmas, as it turned out, came four days early for the lovers of historic buildings in Ste. Genevieve. The bid of Duvall Investments, a company consisting of Orville, Mark and Dr. Joseph Duvall, was accepted. Heartfelt thanks and congratulations poured in from across the preservation community.

The year-long restoration job, carefully done to meet U.S. Department of the Interior specs, was completed in December, 1984 and received a certificate citing the project as "a certified historic structure." The project included constructing a back porch, deck and frame work as it probably would have been in the nineteenth century.

Today the Stanton Building houses an insurance agency, and the Jaccard Building a candy and gift shop. With the attractive Marie Laporte house(circa 1830) next door to the Jaccard Building, and the German Lutheran Church to the east, the charm of Market Street continues from the square, almost to the back yard of the Bolduc-LeMeilleur House at Market and Main.

Until We Meet Again

The historic St. Gemme Stone House, located just south of the city limits on Hwy. 61, met with an unusual fate in 1991 as it was gradually engulfed by Gegg Excavating. When the current generation of ownership took over the company, it was decided that the abandoned house had to go. To the firm's credit, adequate time was given for the stones and massive truss timbers to be surveyed, marked, numbered and carefully disassembled. The components are safely stored, awaiting an appropriate time and place to be reassembled into the significant circa 1799 stone house.

The town of Ste. Genevieve might never have been founded had there not been a vague urging—what we in the twentieth century might call "progress"—prodding Kaskaskia farmers to reach for something a little bit better. Likewise, had the urge to improve their lot not driven the flood-weary colonists up the hill from *le grand champ* in the 1780s and '90s, no Ste. Genevieve would exist today.

That same natural drive to improve one's property and to elevate one's standard of living, also led to the continual destruction of old structures and their replacement with newer, more modern buildings.

What causes angst in the Ste. Genevieve saga is that a large number of significant structures from colonial times (and shortly thereafter) still survived at the turn of the twentieth century, only to be lost within the past 60 years. As the city makes its plans for growth in the 21st Century, redefining "progress" for the old town areas is absolutely critical to the uniqueness Ste. Genevieve possesses. Simply resting on the laurels of the already restored homes and neglecting the maintenance of the other significant architectural treasures could be the demise of the charm and historical significance of this town.

What may appear as an eyesore to most, may well contain, beneath its layers of aging additions, a log structure or a historically or culturally significant link—such as those at 215 and 205 Washington. It is hoped that home and shop owners, landlords, renters, and those who own vacant houses within the historic district will take pride in the treasures they possess, not removing any pieces that belong to the character of the house or the property, and keeping vigil to prevent termite and water damage at the very least.

The old houses take us back to a different era, a glimpse back into time, a time to learn from the past, and to see where we've come to…the real treasure of antiquity. *—mle,psn*

FLOODS

Every lifelong resident of a river community knows the feeling. The river is on the rise. Since the very beginning, Ste. Genevieve has been engaged in a love-hate relationship with the Mississippi. There would be no Ste. Genevieve if it were not for the river. Yet without protection from the Mississippi, there might cease to be a Ste. Genevieve.

No one really knows how high the water was in Old Ste. Genevieve during the flood of 1785, known in local history as *l'année des grandes eaux*. The water was high enough to cover all the homes along the river bank, convincing most residents that an eventual move to higher ground was inevitable. There was, at that time, no official method of comparing flood water levels—all we have is one gentleman's testimony that "in the Big Field the water in many places was twelve or fifteen feet deep."

By the time of the great flood of 1844, engineers devised a method of measuring the water level in order to gather comparison data. At each riverside community, an arbitrary river level was chosen as the "zero" mark to indicate the "normal" depth of the river. Rising waters are guaged at each community in reference to an established "flood stage"—the level at which the river overflows its traditional banks and begins to threaten low-lying areas. The flood stage at Ste. Genevieve is 27 feet above the arbitrary "0" mark.

During the twentieth century, however, a shallower river bed and more paving and levees upstream have played havoc with the traditional flood plain.

Every generation has had to deal with some aspect of flooding—some floods more poignant than others. As if wartime rationing and concerns for the safety of loved ones overseas were not enough to worry families on the home front during World War II, the Mississippi proved to be no patriot. Three straight years from 1942 through 1944 the river flooded, topping out at 39.14 feet. As always, the low-lying areas were hit hard.

Washington Street was underwater between North Main and Third Streets, with the bridges over the North Gabouri threatened with flooding. Many gardens and crops were lost—especially painful during the war-time shortages.

The first 40-foot floods since 1844 hit in

1947 (40.26) and 1951 (40.28). The 1951 Fair Play reported that all of Main Street from Washington north to Little Rock was under water; Washington from Front street to a half-block west of Third; North Second to Jefferson; South Main; Jefferson from Front to Second; Third from Jefferson to LaHaye; LaHaye from Third back to the bend. Some 50,000 acres of land in the Big Field and Cotton Woods were under water. —mle

The Flood of 1973

For another two decades, the St. Louis flood gauge did not reach 34 feet. The river made up for lost time in 1973, however. A new generation of Ste. Genevievens discovered what Jean Baptiste Vallé twice lived through.

Although footage-wise this crest was not as high as was reached in 1951, marks put on buildings in that year by area residents had disappeared early in the week under the murky waters even though gauge readings were well below those of 1951. The crest finally hit on April 28, 1973 at a whopping 43.31 feet.

National guardsmen and local residents worked day and night in desperate sandbagging operations. The levees held and most of Ste. Genevieve was spared. Sadly, one local teenager died during the ordeal, falling from the back of a pickup while hauling sandbags. She is believed to have been the city's only 20th Century flood fatality.

That summer, rumors of a monster 50-foot crest began spreading. What would have sounded ludicrous a year earlier, now seemed eerily possible. Talk of a 50-footer was eventually forgotten—by everyone but the Mississippi. —mle

The Christmas Flood of 1982

Floods can come at any time, during any season. Generally speaking, however, river residents have felt relatively safe during the winter months. Melting snow upriver, along with annual spring rains, usually make spring the most common flood season. The great river, however, knows no calendar. Thanksgiving 1982 was dampened only slightly by a week-long rain. Valle High School won its third consecutive Class 2A state football championship that weekend and few anticipated anything other than a peaceful holiday season in the old town. The holiday mood was marred in early December, however, as the rain continued and the North and South Gabouri branches began climbing out of their banks. When the creeks began backing up on December 4, it became apparent that Ste. Genevieve had a problem. Soon the low-lying areas of town were inundated for the third time in a decade. Sandbaggers beheld the eerie sight of Christmas lights reflected in flood water outside houses decorated for the usually festive season. —mle

Ode to the Nightwatch

Anonymous figure of the night
Keeping vigil in this precarious Venician setting
'Tis the pump watchman
Sleepless as the rising waters.

Seasonal lights dance across the fluid desert
Warming the heart of his frozen exterior
Hurriedly he builds his fire
Three feet below its placid mirror.

The drone of his pump chatters in the
crisp winter chill,
A soothing lullaby to those in their homes,
To him a fearful earth rumbling
To them a fear unknown.

Bill Naeger, 1982

The Flood of 1993

Nothing could have been finer in Ste. Genevieve in the early spring of 1993. Still basking in the glory and state-wide recognition of a double state football championship by the Class 1A Valle Warriors and the Class 3A Ste. Genevieve Dragons, the old French town was also seeing its tourism industry grow in vitality with each passing year.

In fact, in his 1985 masterwork, *Colonial Ste. Genevieve*, Dr. Carl J. Ekberg remarked that "Life in Ste. Genevieve is no longer continuously influenced by the presence of the Mississippi River. Levees have largely tamed the destructive forces of the river...The routine of daily life in modern Ste. Genevieve would not be materially altered if the town were located ten miles inland."

Prior to 1993, the river had reached official flood stage in the month of April fourteen different years. When the April flood in '93 threatened, the levee district was well prepared. In the years after the Christmas flood of '82, the levee district had expanded the levee so that closure on both sides of the Third Street bridge and the North Main bridge were possible and quickly executed. This would protect areas of Main, Washington, Third and LaHaye that had not been under levee protection previously. The low-lying areas in the city such as Front and North Main Streets would fall to their usual watery fate.

The Spring flood of '93 reached a crest of 37.7 feet and by the end of May, the barricades were taken down and clean-up proceeded as usual.

AT LEFT: The Valle schoolyard became the hub of sandbagging operations in the central district.

AT RIGHT: Levee captains and concerned citizens gather for one of several emergency management noon meetings.

It was ironic that in late June the city received word from Washington that it had been denied federal assistance to help cover the cost of the April flood fight. The Corps of Engineers, at the same time, revealed that they had not found sufficient cause for reducing the required local matching funds for the construction of a federal levee to protect the town. A grass roots effort was begun to look into the feasibility of a locally backed levee project.

In the midst of all this, Ste. Genevieve was named as one of "America's Eleven Most Endangered Historic Places" by the National Trust for Historic Preservation. It cited the community's "plague of periodic flooding" and "lack of resources to preserve its historically significant buildings" as reasons to be included in the annual listing.

At the city board meeting on June 24 there was some discussion, among other topics, of the predictions of high water. The board decided to secure extra pumps and agreed to consider the levee district's request for $4000 to study the possibility of a locally backed levee. It was to be the last *regular* board meeting for seven weeks. On July 1, city and levee district officials had the first of what was to become their daily noon emergency meetings. The river stage was 32.5 with predictions calling for a crest of 39 to 40 feet.—*mle*

The crew and passengers of the Mississippi and Delta Queen riverboats celebrated with townspeople at the Fourth of July festivities in the park. Unable to get into St. Louis due to the high water, the boats had docked at Ste. Genevieve's Marina de Gabouri after their annual race. As the boats pulled away from their moorings on July 5, Ste. Genevieve waved goodbye to the last leisurely day it would know for two months.

An all out effort was mounted and most citizens rallied to the call putting aside thoughts of all else but to join in the battle to save the town. Out-of-town volunteers soon came to understand where the Valle schoolyard got its nickname. The "Desert" became a hub of the sandbagging operation in the center of town, as did the VFW lot for the soon-to-be-cut-off north end of town. In searing 100 degree temperatures, sandbaggers labored to fill bags with screenings from Mississippi Lime Company. The readily available tailings were instrumental to the success of the effort as was the stone quarried from Tower Rock Stone just north of town.

Church bells tolled from the Ste. Genevieve Catholic Church, as sandbaggers continued shoveling screenings into burlap bags under the sweltering noonday sun.

People came from various cities and states—many using their vacation time—to help with some aspect of the flood fight. The tasks of filling or throwing sandbags became less tedious for locals when sharing the work with the newcomers.

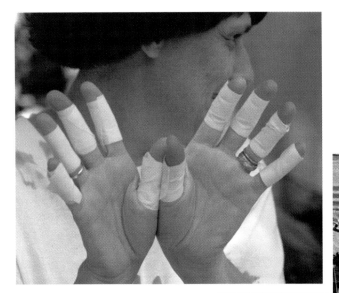

DESERT COMMAND POST

When Governor Mel Carnahan declared Ste. Genevieve a disaster area, the National Guard was deployed to assist in the fight. The town was suddenly transformed into a virtual battle zone. Helicopters routinely circled overhead, humvees plowed through flooded roads, military police patrolled the streets and Guardsmen threw sandbags with civilians—all becoming part of the town's daily life.

The town was divided into strategic sections under the supervision of civilian and rotating military personnel. Louis Sexauer, Gary LaRose and Tim Uding took charge of the areas beyond the North Gabouri Creek; Alvin Donze, Walt Timm and Vernon Schwent oversaw the activity in the central section; Jerry Roth and Emerald Loida spearheaded the effort in the St. Mary Road and marina area. The entire project was coordinated by Levee District III President Vernon Bauman and the county's Emergency Preparedness Director Mick Schwent.

The levee eventually stretched over three miles and rose to more than twenty feet in some places. As the Ste. Genevieve Herald reported "It grew and shifted like something alive in response to daily conditions and river predictions."

Many of the homes along North Main began the fight with a new innovation—concrete highway barriers along with sandbags—but fell victim to the river before emergency action moved into full swing. Early efforts to protect a portion of Lahaye and Biltmore along the North Gabouri failed after the 42 foot river stage pushed the water over the barriers.

The city issued an evacuation order for potentially threatened areas as early as July 7. The Post Office relocated its operation to an abandoned grocery store on the corner of US 61 and Highway M. The downtown area, protected but evacuated, had a haunting stillness. The area was patrolled by the Dublin, Ohio police and the only sound in the steamy afternoons was that of the constant drone of pumps.

Owners and employee sit in an evacuated Hotel Ste. Genevieve following a police order which shut down many businesses in the downtown historic district. The area was ultimately spared from inundation.

The Red Cross took over the business of feeding volunteers, displaced families and military workers as well as providing tetanus booster shots to sandbaggers. Originally housed in the basement of the downtown Baptist Church, the operation was moved to high ground at the American Legion Hall. Those unable to sandbag worked night and day to feed and deliver refreshments to famished volunteers. The VFW Hall became a second feeding location when the floodwaters closed the Fourth Street bridge. The closing divided the town into the North and the South, leaving the only access to the north a fifteen minute drive via the Industrial Road.

The city's water supply was contaminated by floodwater which had covered the city's well system by the third week of July. Cans and jugs of water were donated for drinking, and until temporary shower facilities were installed at the Ste. Genevieve High School and the city pool, most of the city residents had to depend on county friends and family.

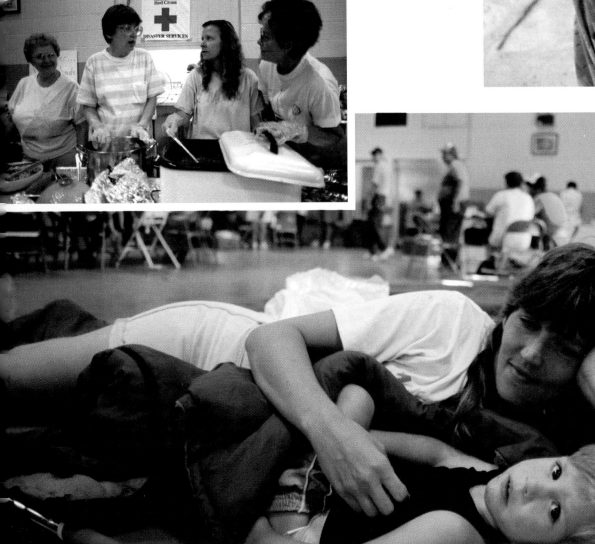

Already heavy into the thrust of the fight, it seemed there was no turning back when crest predictions in mid-July changed from under 43 to over 47 feet. Levee walkers, throughout the day and night, kept vigil on any trouble spots, seeps or sand boils. By the end of July, the predicted crest was 49 feet. "Two or three weeks ago," admitted Levee District President Vern Bauman, "if somebody had told us it would go to 49 feet, I don't think we'd be here fighting. I believe we'd have grabbed what we could and ran."

A decision was made in mid-July to close the Fourth Street bridge across the North Gabouri Creek. Although closing the bridge meant that access to and from the north end of town now required a 15 minute drive via the Industrial Road, it opened the creek channel in the event of a flash flood. On July 23, the decision proved to be a wise one when the skies opened and dropped several inches of rain in 30 minutes. A surge of water roared through the now open passage. Sandbaggers worked frantically to contain the swelling torrents—even forming a human wall with bodies and plastic sheeting at one point to hold back the water. The event prompted Levee District President Vern Bauman to exclaim, "We'll win it or lose it right here in the next hour."

The effect of the flash flood was felt in other parts of town as well. The South Gabouri swelled, temporarily inundating neighborhoods as far west as Seventh Street and washing a section of pavement from Chadwell Lane. The Knights of Columbus Hall appeared to have a moat around its fine granite walls. In some places, rainwater run-off was trapped behind private levees at a higher level than that on the outside of the levee.

The North Gabouri bridge at Fourth and LaHaye prior to its closing.

Vern Bauman and Emerald Loida watch helplessly as the Valle Spring Levee crumbles under the pressure of the Mississippi River.

On August 1, an urgent call came into the noon emergency meeting at city hall. A fissure had developed in a section of the Valle Spring Levee—a secondary levee which protected several residences, businesses, and the historic homes on St. Mary Road. Responding to the call, levee captains determined that the slide was not nearly so serious as one sand boil—of several—which had developed behind the levee. An heroic attempt was made to ring the trouble spot with bags as the churning boil spewed up ever-increasing amounts of earth-laden water. But in minutes a geyser was spouting from the hole, undermining the base of the levee. The levee crumbled into the raging water, taking with it a flatbed truck which had hauled sandbags to the site. In desperation, levee captain Vern Bauman positioned his earth-moving equipment on the levee attempting to fill in the ever-widening gap. It was a losing battle. Bauman backed his equipment off the levee and watched helplessly with others as the river claimed its territory. Across the Big Field basin, residents saw the encroaching water advance steadily. By mid-afternoon the water level had equalized, but not before flooding homes and businesses. After watching levees all along the Mississippi fall like dominoes, Ste. Genevieve had suffered its first major—and only—failure in its massive emergency levee system.

The Valle Spring Levee break—chronicled in a locally-produced documentary—would be the only major breach in Ste. Genevieve's extensive levee system during the flood of 1993.

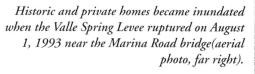

M and S Meat Packing, before and after the Valle Spring Levee break.

Historic and private homes became inundated when the Valle Spring Levee ruptured on August 1, 1993 near the Marina Road bridge(aerial photo, far right).

August 4th and 5th are remembered as two of the most fragile days of the fight. The Silvanus levee protecting the downtown area was experiencing near disasters. A private levee protecting several homes on Highway 61 just south of town failed. An emergency call for help at the historic home of Frank and Shirley Myers brought civilians and guardsmen out to squelch a potential disaster.

The sandbag levee at the home of Ishmael and Elaine Scherer experienced a wall collapse in the early hours of the morning when a pump failed. The Scherer home had come to symbolize, to the watching world, the poignant battle in which the town was engaged. Just one block from City Hall—through which all media crews were routed—the home was easily accessed by news teams. The gracious hospitality and expressive faith which they found there was conveyed over airwaves to millions throughout the country. Volunteers from around the nation shared in the town's struggle through the media and consequently were moved from their television sets to the sandbag fields of Ste. Genevieve. Early on, the motto "We Can Do This!" became the rallying cry. But as news spread of levees collapsing in other river townships, it became evident that any success would ultimately be by the grace of God.

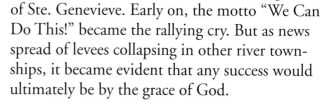

The crest of 49.67 feet occurred August 6 on a mild sunny day. The town was quiet. After so many changing crests, perhaps the townsfolk didn't want to get their hopes up only to be disappointed by yet another crest prediction. But this time, however, the crest proved to be final.

The Burlap Wall
SERAPHIN and St MARY'S Rd.
Ste Genevieve, Mo.

WELCOME
TO
LAKE
S. MAIN

WE DIDN'T
REST UNTIL
IT CREST

As the waters receded, the flood-weary community had yet another task to face—that of cleaning up the mess that the river had left behind. But like angels, out-of-town volunteers continued to pour into town to assist in the stenchy and mucky work of flood clean-up.

The summer was nearly over. School would begin on schedule August 27. It was a summer of inundated baseball fields and barely any baseball. The municipal band had ended its season on the Fourth of July. There was little time for vacations, swimming or leisurely backyard bar-be-ques. The town's largest festival, the Jour de Fête, was cancelled. There was a challenge at hand and everyone took part in the victory. For even with the failures, the overall picture was one of amazing success.

—bn,psn

As unimaginable as the 1993 flood was in its proportion, the common belief that it was a "fluke" and a "500-year flood" proved to be dubious two years later. Just as the town was digging out of the muck and mire and governmental red tape of 1993, the town was besieged by the second-worst flood in city history! This time the crest topped the 45-foot mark—two feet higher than the monster 1973 flood. However, with most of the levee still intact from '93, the city was able to accomplish protection from the encroaching waters with comparative ease.

Many long-held opinions had to be re-thought after the 1993 and 1995 floods. For one, the Mississippi flood plain had changed—whether one cared to admit it or not. What were once considered safe sites to build on, now had to be considered no-build areas.

Many residents took advantage of a Federal Emergency Management Association (FEMA) buyout program—especially along flood-ravaged North Main. —mle

In the Wake of the Flood

One positive effect of the flood of 1993 was the increased national exposure–especially regarding the importance of Ste. Genevieve's historic architecture and culture.

The flood also cemented French, French-Canadian and Franco-American support for the besieged town. When a number of radio talk shows began blasting the French for not helping fight to preserve the threatened French Colonial heritage, noted author Charles J. Balesi had a brain storm.

FROM LEFT: Madame Yves Gaudeul; Mayor Wm. Anderson; Elizabeth Gentry Sayad, Mo. Chairman of French Heritage Relief Committee; Meade Summers, Jr., Vice Chairman FHR Com.; Robert Mecker, President, Foundation for Restoration of Ste. Genevieve; Yves Gaudeul, Consul General of France; Charles Balesi.

The author of *The Time of the French in the Heart of North America, 1673-1818,* Balesi contacted Consul General of France, Yves Gaudeul and got the ball rolling. With strong support from the Franco-American communities of Chicago and St. Louis they formed the French Heritage Relief Committee, which would be dissolved once the committee's goals had been met.

Until the committee could obtain tax-exempt status, it worked with the National Trust for Historic Preservation, which was seeking a partner with which to protect the French Historical Mississippi Corridor. The committee received its tax exempt status in January, 1994.

Gaudeul was able to interest Princess Marie-Sol de La Tour d'Auvergne, president of the Friends of the Vieilles Maisons Françaises

in the project. The princess subsequently spoke at a number of events to help raise money and awareness for the threatened French heritage.

The committee then purchased the c.1792 Amoureux House from the Donze Estate in Ste. Genevieve and donated it to the State of Missouri for future safekeeping. Excess Missouri funds went to Ste. Genevieve for tourism projects. Illinois funds went to repairing the badly damaged 1740 Kaskaskia Bell.

By the time the French Heritage Relief Committee had disbanded, it had pumped over $120,000 into Ste. Genevieve, including just under $88,000 to buy the Amoureux House.

The committee legally ceased to exist on August 15, 1995, its work completed. Elizabeth Gentry Sayad and a number of St. Louis supporters of French heritage then founded *Les Amis*, "The Friends," a French heritage preservation group, which has remained active in promoting and preserving Missouri's French history.

In 1997, work began on an urban design levee which, upon its completion, holds the promise of protecting Ste. Genevieve from the ravages of the river. Tourism and other industry is flourishing again and local residents only occasionally take a glimpse over their shoulder in the direction of the mighty river.

Even when she stays in her banks, the mighty Mississippi is an impossible presence to ignore.—*mle*

Ste. Genevieve Remains

An old tire swing hangs aimlessly
From a tired, bitter branch.
The matted rope holds on,
    Like so many nerve ends exposed
To the elements.

The wind tosses and turns it in
    turmoil,
Taunting its vulnerability.

Memories of children grasping
Tightly with white knuckles,
Like the stains on the clapboard
From intruding muddy waters.

The man-made mountain stands tall
    Like a monument
On the shores of the battlefield,
Where many lives were lost,
And many dreams,
    Submerged into oblivian.

Mary Ellen Ladd, 1996

Ste. Genevieve

Live

People
Traditions
Seasons

"Bonsoir, le maître et la maîtresse
et tout le monde du logis.
O pour le dernier jour de l'année,
La Guillannée vous nous devez."

Thus begins the song addressing the master and mistress of the house. The custom in the early days of Ste. Genevieve was to travel from house to house singing *La Guiannée* and dancing the accompanying shuffling step. The song continues on to ask for a big piece of beef, or if that not be possible, then the oldest daughter with which to dance away the night. In the continuing tradition of the early French settlers, *La Guignolée* is performed each New Year's Eve in most of the town's public places, restaurants and bars for all to enjoy.

La Guignolée or La Guiannée?

"I can not understand a word of it," exclaimed a visiting writer from France. However, after following the Guignolée the entire New Year's Eve, she had to admit, "It does not matter—they are so much fun."

Anglo and Germanic accents have overtaken the pronunciation of the original French words of the song, but *joie de vivre* is the spirit of the troupe—decidedly French. Most of the performers can trace their ancestry back to the original French inhabitants—LaRose, Moreau, Papin, Maurice, Labruyere, Beauchamp and Lalumondiere. But others, offering no excuses simply identify themselves as "Krauts in French clothing."

La Guillannée (locally pronounced "gee-oh´-nee" with a hard "g") performs every New Year's Eve and has ever since the earliest arrivals from French Canada in the mid-1700s. Performing for the public at Valle High School and the nursing homes, they continue the evening singing at the halls, restaurants and bars. La Guiannée has, through the years, travelled on foot, horse-drawn carriage, schoolbus, and most recently by charter bus making the tradition quite curious. During the war years,

when so many men were away, the women even broke the all-men tradition in order to keep the Guignolée alive (bottom photo, next page). La Guiannée dress in top hats and long-tailed tuxedos, as monks, trappers, Indians, French gentry, clowns, and even Keystone cops. They dance a shuffling little step encircling the fiddlers and principal *chanteur*.

The spelling of La Guignolée has been questioned over the years—the derivation of the word itself not fully understood. After much debate preceeding the 1935 Bicentennial Celebration of Ste. Genevieve, the word Guignolée was adopted, based on the name of a clownish band of revellers and carousers in a New York City theater. Cast aside was the proposed spelling Gaie-Année (happy year), Guiannée or Guillannée both having their roots in an ancient Druid custom of collecting the mistletoe or *gui* to use in the rights of spring. The curious thing about accepting Guignolée as the correct word is that it is seldom pronounced

(geen-nyo-lay) as it is spelled. Also, the word Guignolée has no reference to celebrating the new year. So for that reason, we here continue to use all spellings randomly in keeping with the custom's other ironies and leave it to the reader to decide. None-theless—whether Guignolée or Guiannée, horse-drawn buggy or charter bus, fur trapper or Keystone cop—townspeople and visitors alike would feel the season incomplete without Ste. Genevieve's oldest living tradition.

⚜ The King's Ball ⚜

Characters from the past—a monk, a medieval princess, a French nobleman with an Indian squaw, a Scotsman and a French peasant girl—arrive at the hall, their assumed French names announced as they enter. The caller begins the evening with the Grande Promenade and soon the fiddler strikes up the more lively dances—squares, reels, circles and lines. Costumed dancers laugh in the merriment of the dance unconcerned that an old French custom from earliest colonial days is being re-enacted. For some, this is the second King's Ball of the year, having attended the ball in Prairie du Rocher, Illinois on the Saturday closest to Twelfth Night. Ste. Genevieve's *Le Bal du Roi* is held on the first Saturday in February, falling traditionally somewhere between Twelfth Night (Epiphany) and Ash Wednesday which begins the Lenten fasting.

Midway through the evening, music and dancing cease as the men—or women on leap years—choose a piece of spice cake. The lucky

men finding the bean in the cake become the court along with their ladies. The gent who discovers the plastic Christ child in his piece is crowned the King of the Ball. A royal procession follows, and gifts and song are bestowed upon the royalty. The King and Queen are honored by presiding over parades and community events throughout the year.

The Tastes of Tradition

Bouillon

Aside from La Guiannée and Le Bal du Roi(The King's Ball), the living traditions of the French have, with only a few exceptions, been teutonized. However, the French soup, bouillon, fell into such favor with the German arrivals to this French village that it has become a mainstay in Ste. Genevieve cooking.

The Red Cross blood drives which are held at the American Legion, V.F.W., or Knights of Columbus halls serve the savory, clear chicken broth and the chicken salad sandwiches made from the stock source to the blood donors. Deliciously welcome after giving blood, one can almost feel the red blood cells rebuilding. This is tradition at its finest.

The recipe is simple. A good stewing hen—some swear the older the better—is covered in a large pot with water and boiled along with onions, cabbage, carrots, celery, and sometimes turnips and seasoned with salt and pepper. The longer the hen is simmered, the richer the stock. The broth is strained and served in a mug with the vegetables and chicken served on a platter as a side dish. Some refrigerate the stock until they can skim off the fat. Others testify to the "healing" qualities of leaving the fat in.

The Friday White Meal

French or German, if you were Catholic prior to the late 1960s, Friday was a meatless day. If you were lucky enough to catch them, or wealthy enough to buy them, you ate fish. Many, however, made due with the ingredients on hand—flour and eggs to make noodles, potatoes to dice and boil with onions, and dry white beans soaked overnight and cooked with salt and pepper, maybe some cabbage and onion. This meal was known to many as the Friday meal. Stewed tomatoes or stewed prunes over the white meal provided a little color, not to mention flavor. Those marrying into a family with this seemingly bland, starchy meal may wonder what the fuss is all about. Those having grown up with it, however, talk of it as if it were a feast fit for a king. Although many today may buy store-bought noodles and canned beans to make the meal, the real magic was probably in watching grandma roll and cut out the noodles, giving little bits of the raw dough to the children. The Friday meal is comfort food at its best and can be appreciated even without the experience of its rich tradition. The meal is served in most of the downtown restaurants along with fried fish every Friday.

BACKGROUND PHOTO: The Friday white meal—Ste. Genevieve soul food

Liver Dumplings

Ste. Genevieve's signature food must indisputably be liver dumplings, a dish unique to the county's particular German heritage. The parish picnic dinners in Zell, Weingarten, Ozora and Lawrenceton would not be complete without the knaeflies. Each of the downtown restaurants serve fried chicken, mashed potatoes and gravy, and liver dumplings one day of the week as their special. And on Sundays the meal is expanded to also include dressing, sauerkraut and green beans. Liver knaeflies are made by most families for the holidays and special occasions. It's definitely a food that declares "this is a special day!"

Although flour, eggs, liver, and seasonings are the main ingredients, there are so many variations that Ste. Genevieve's popular Valle Cookbook lists seven different recipes for the knaeflies.

Well-known Ste. Genevieve cook Anna Eisenbeis has been making liver knaeflies for over 60 years. She learned the recipe from her mother who learned it from her mother. Catering the dish for trail rides and receptions, she says she has made as many as 20 gallons in one day. Her basic recipe, which she willingly volunteers, serves 75 people. "If you want to make less, you'll have to break it down yourself!"

TOP PHOTO: Scratching liver dumplings into boiling water at the Zell Fall Festival
BOTTOM PHOTO: Liver knaeflies are part of the Tuesday special at the Hotel Ste. Genevieve

Oberle Sausage

Jack and Bill Oberle with a rack of their famous Oberle Sausage.

ABOVE: Joseph and Bernadine Oberle sit between their youngest, Fred and John, c.1896. In back are August, Katherine, George, William and Lena.
RIGHT: Chris Cabral with former employer Jerry Oberle and a butcher block of succulent treats in 1984.
BELOW: A young Butch Callier(left) stands with his cousin, Buddy, in his uncle John Oberle's shop at 123 Merchant Street, c.1935.

ABOVE: Brothers John, Fred and August pose in their father's shop on Main Street, c.1915. RIGHT: A young Tim Arnold pulls a rack of his grandpa Oberle "Butch" Callier's sausage out of the smoker in 1984.

When Joseph and Bernadine Oberle brought their family to Ste. Genevieve in 1871, little did they know that five generations later the family name would bear trademark status along with the family recipe for their succulent smoked sausage. To savor a slice of Oberle sausage today—or "dog" as it is known locally—is to sample a 120 year tradition of family butchering.

Joseph first set up shop in his residence on North Main Street. The original smokehouse still stands. Joseph passed along the family recipe to each of his children, most of whom picked up the meat cleaver to carry on the family tradition. With each generation, the family sausage recipe was passed down, with slight refinements and embellishments added as each son, nephew or cousin improved his own version. At one point in the 1980s, four different neighborhood meat markets were selling the popular sausage—each owned by one of Joseph and Bernadine's descendents.

Experimenting with the recipe has not been beyond any of the descendents either and has given rise to some unusual offshoots of the traditional sausage. Deer hunters regularly have their venison ground and made into "deer dog." Siblings Tim Arnold and Patti Klein, fifth generation Oberles who now own and operate their grandpa "Butch" Callier's Meat Market, say that some of the more unusual combinations which they have ground and seasoned with the family herbs for private orders have included raccoon, goat or beaver meat.

In the 1970s, the Oberle sausage legacy gained momentum when Joseph's great-grandson Jack Oberle began vacuum packing his brand and distributing it regionally. Vacuum packed Oberle sausage has been enjoyed in the fields of Vietnam and in Desert Storm. Following in his father's entrepreneurial footsteps, Jack's son Bill trademarked the family's smoked meat products in 1994 giving official status to five generations of smoked meats tradition.

To sample a succulent slice of smoked seasoned sausage today is to appreciate five generations of butchering tradition— one might say it's a taste of the local flavor.

Not So Long Ago...

"Baby boomers" can recall when Ste. Genevieve had many rural elements within the confines of its city limits as recently as the 1950s and early '60s. Their grandparents who had survived the first world war, the influenza epidemic of 1918, the Great Depression, and World War II continued to live and pass on the frugal and religious lifestyle which had seen them through the hard times.

Just fifty years ago, hens cackled from the old chicken coops and woodsy odors filled the air from the brick smoke houses which still stand behind many of Ste. Genevieve's homes.

Victory gardens of the war years were maintained, and many town families canned and froze their own fresh produce. Milk, in returnable glass bottles, was delivered to homes in the wee morning hours by the milkman, or bought from farmers, some whose farms were even within the city limits.

Flour, sugar, yeast, and baking powder were the staples bought from the neighborhood grocer, which along with the fresh eggs and milk in the skillful hands of most housewives, were transformed into noodles, biscuits, breads, pies, cakes, and cookies.

A predominently Catholic town, most homes were modestly decorated with crucifixes, religious prints, and Blessed Virgin lawn ornaments. The Catholic Mass, delivered in Latin with the priest's back to the congregation, was central to the daily lives of most parishioners. Women would not enter church without a head covering, and men always removed their hats. The church was open for daily devotions, confessions, lighting the votive candles or praying the Rosary. The Sisters of St. Joseph, who taught at Valle, could be seen daily, walking single file in procession in their long black and white habits on their way to 6 a.m. Mass.

Grandparents told of the days when they fished the clear-running Gabouri Creeks and picnicked on their banks. One of the drawbacks of the fifties, however, was a lack of environmental consciousness. The South Gabouri Creek, at that time, was thick and white with lime sludge. Today, once again, the creek runs almost as clear as the old timers remembered it.

Although as early as the 1930's, gas stations began springing up on nearly every block in the old town, many residents considered it a luxury to own a car. Lime kiln workers were transported by school bus to work, there were two taxi cab services, every neighborhood had at least one grocery store, and Koetting's Supermarket even delivered groceries to homes free of charge.

Downtown promotions, such as Rozier's Tuf-Nut Days, and sidewalk and Moonlight Madness sales were part of the "shop at home" incentive, an almost unheard of value in today's commuter, computer and global economy. The philosophy was deeply ingrained—support each other's business instead of shopping out of town and it would all come back in forms of community spirit, town improvements and returned support.

But change was in the air for the old town by the mid-'60s. Within the Catholic community the effects of Vatican II would filter in—the Mass would be said in English and the priest would face the congregation, Fridays would no longer be meatless, and the dress of most of the Sisters of St. Joseph would resemble modest secular street clothing.

As more women joined the work force, two-car families would soon be the norm. With this increased mobility, the neighborhood grocery store would find itself having to compete with out-of-town shopping marts and be expected to carry more inventory in the way of quick preparation and frozen foods.

In 1966, Koetting's grocery, one of the largest of the downtown neighborhood grocers, bought out its closest competitor just one block away—the Clover Farm store. After 81 years on the square, feeling the need to modernize, Koetting's left the downtown area in 1972 and moved to the new shopping center on Highway 61.

The shopping center with its easy access and parking, contributed to the identity crisis which is felt in the downtown area even to the present. Ste. Genevieve, however, retains enough of its rural and small town traditions, family-owned businesses, and remnants of the past to remind a hometowner or visitor of a not-so-long-ago, but quite different past.

A Merchandising Tradition
Koetting's

Ste. Genevieve commerce is rich with family run businesses that make up another facet of the community's varied and congenial personality. With the slogan "Since 1887" the Koetting family enterprise can legitimately be called the oldest continuously operated family business in Ste. Genevieve.*

The Koetting family, as they are known today, are musicians, actors, artists, and business people who dabble in electronics, computers, photography, sewing, video, old cars, golf—well, in essence, there isn't much that doesn't capture their imagination. But at Koetting's Foodway you'll find them stocking shelves, running promotions and ads, bookkeeping, managing, and checking out groceries. In other words...chips off the old block.

Born in Hollig, Germany in 1856, John Koetting immigrated with his family to the United States at age nine. He apprenticed with a shoe maker in Linn, Missouri when he was 14 and opened his own shoe repair business in Bonnet's Mill, Missouri at age twenty. Studying watch repair in St. Louis, he then set up his own jewelry store in Ste. Genevieve in 1887. Four years later, he added musical instruments, particularly Estay pianos to his inventory and learned to play them. At that time, he was renting a building owned by Dr. Carssow for his business but soon bought the property next door owned by the Guion's on Market Street.

A Renaissance man, he learned to speak French, send messages by telegraph, studied

At the time of the second printing of this book in late 1999, Koetting's Foodway had been sold, thus ending this long family tradition.

astronomy and clock repair, and learned to tune organs and pianos. Buying a stock of coffins, he became one of the first licensed undertakers in Missouri.

His wife ran a millinery shop with her sister out of the expanding business, now extended into a new building he had built after buying and tearing down the Zeiser building. Within this building was not only groceries, furniture, and a men's clothing department,

but the first floor was dedicated to a short-lived venture in the 1920s—the Lyric Theatre. There the talents of his children were put to work. They formed the orchestra which accompanied the silent films.

By the time the Lyric ended its not-too-profitable career, Koetting's was a general store with dry goods, women's clothing, shoes, hardware, gift items, notions, kerosene and poultry.

As John Koetting's family and trusted employees were able to run satisfactorily his new ventures, he went back to watch making and public relations.

It is said he spoke English without an accent, could converse in French with the Frenchmen, and speak the Badish dialect with the Germans. He participated in amateur dramatics, was on the school board, a volunteer fireman, and sang with the La Guiannée.

The story continues in its fourth generation in the form of Koetting's Foodway without a break from generation to generation. One great-grandson is creating his own tradition, branching out into outdoor power equipment with his offspring.

Family-owned businesses have been the hallmark of communities since the birth of free enterprise. Success was measured by the degree of honest, personal service a business could provide, as well as the bottom line of the ledger book. Competition from mass merchandisers make it possible for today's consumer to have "more for less" at the expense of something less tangible—the community spirit derived from the well-run family business.

One of Ste. Genevieve's oldest continuously-operating business families—the Koetting clan poses in 1972 during the grand opening of their new location at Pointe Basse Plaza.

The End of an Era

When Rozier's, a family-owned and operated store, closed its doors for good in 1995, a feeling of great loss and perhaps doom set upon those concerned about the survival of downtown Ste. Genevieve.

Beginning in 1811 with the arrival of Ferdinand Rozier and John James Audubon and 200 barrels of whiskey to sell or trade, the Rozier merchandising tradition had begun. Long known as the dime store and the east side as the clothing store, by the 1980s, Rozier's in downtown Ste. Genevieve was selling everything from furniture to groceries, from nuts and bolts to bolts of material, from lawnmowers to fashionable clothing, and from sporting gear to video sales and rentals. It had become the one-stop shop downtown.

Competition from superstores within a 40-mile radius on every side but the river, however, spelled trouble. In an increasingly mobile town, it seemed Roziers would have to compensate by being open late hours, Sundays and holidays. They did this for a number of years, the Rozier boys still managing to coach youth soccer and basketball games. The flood of 1993 took a heavy toll on the business with the virtual shutdown of the downtown area. It began to seem apparent that it was a losing battle. Along with the employees, they made the decision to close. The building went up for sale in 1995 and family members and employees went on to find other employment. One stockholder, Herbert "Jack" Myers, Jr., whose father had helped open Roziers in downtown Ste. Genevieve, went on to open his own shoe store in the historic district.

Although a very large antique mall occupies the immense space, the loss of such a diverse store causes many to question the fate of the downtown area.

Getting to Know You

Even with the changes, downtown Ste. Genevieve remains a vital place with real life action. It's not easy getting from place to place in a hurry. Whether it's dropping a letter off at the post office, paying an electric bill, placing a yard sale ad in the newspaper, voting at the courthouse, getting a hair cut, or doughnuts from the bakery, you're bound to run into someone who needs to talk to you or just wants to chat.

Sure, it's a town full of intriguing antique and craft shops, as well as its museum houses, fine restaurants, beautiful bed and breakfasts, candy shop, and its own winery—but what sets it apart from other tourist towns is its people and family connections.

Outsiders moving into Ste. Genevieve have been baffled to find that the first thing locals want to establish is, "Who are you related to?"

It's a deep-rooted family town with many family-related activities—weddings, anniversaries, funerals, church events, etc.—sometimes making a new-comer feel excluded and wondering what there is to do in Ste. Genevieve. Those that succeed in making Ste. Genevieve their home, have generally done so by becoming involved in their church, their children's activities, or by joining one of the town's many service or social organizations.

The "everyone-knows-everyone-else's-business" syndrome can, at times, take its toll, but its positive effect is one of accountability. You're not just a nameless face in Ste Genevieve.

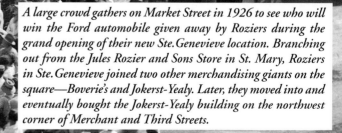

A large crowd gathers on Market Street in 1926 to see who will win the Ford automobile given away by Roziers during the grand opening of their new Ste. Genevieve location. Branching out from the Jules Rozier and Sons Store in St. Mary, Roziers in Ste. Genevieve joined two other merchandising giants on the square—Boverie's and Jokerst-Yealy. Later, they moved into and eventually bought the Jokerst-Yealy building on the northwest corner of Merchant and Third Streets.

Limestone

Limestone has been at the foundation of the Ste. Genevieve county economy for nearly a century. Western Lime Works was in operation as early as 1904 under the ownership of John Tlapek, Henry Rozier and Jules Petrequin. In the 1930s, four different quarries in the area were mining the high-calcium deposits.

Of the three layers which comprise the limestone deposits underlying Ste. Genevieve, it is the 100-feet thick middle layer—known as the Salem or Spurgeon deposit—that is intensively mined today by Mississippi Lime Company and Chemical Lime Company. The vein is unique because of its exceptional purity and consistency—being 98 per cent calcium carbonate. This, along with easy transport of the product afforded by the Mississippi River, gives Ste. Genevieve lime a competitive edge in the marketplace.

Limestone, in both its raw and various refined states, is used in a wide variety of products. It is used in the manufacture of steel, glass, rubber, plastics and paper. Coal-burning plants use it as a desulfurization agent. It is used in water treatment facilities, agriculture, the making of pharmaceuticals and in food processing. —bn

Mississippi Lime Company

Mississippi Lime Company opened its doors in 1912, the same year that saw the first car and airplane enter Ste. Genevieve. It is difficult to ascertain today, which of the three has had a greater effect upon Ste. Genevieve. Since its humble beginning, the company has grown into the most diversified producer of lime products in North America.

The town's largest employer for generations, Mississippi Lime Company has helped the local economy survive two world wars, the Great Depression and other crises, with only a modest degree of distress. Now a sophisticated, modern corporation, Mississippi Lime Company is known for the high quality of lime it produces. This leads to more than one million tons of lime from the Ste. Genevieve plant being shipped nationwide each year.

Founded by Harry B. Mathews, Jr., the company has not only remained locally operated, but has also remained a family business. Now in its third generation of family ownership, Mississippi Lime Company has always been extremely generous in its support of Ste. Genevieve. Harry B. and Constance Mathews were among the first individuals to take steps to preserve the town's unique and endangered French Colonial architectural legacy. Many of the historic restorations in town benefited either directly or indirectly from Mississippi Lime support. The company continues to support a wide range of worthwhile local programs, including a scholarship fund for both local high schools. *—mle*

ABOVE: The Valle High School Band during a homecoming parade.
ABOVE, RIGHT: Dixieland Express performs during the Fall Festival.
RIGHT: Ste. Genevieve High School Band at the Thanksgiving Day Parade in St. Louis.
BELOW: The Ste. Genevieve German Band can be heard during Jour de Fete and the Fall Festival.

The Ste. Genevieve Municipal Band

"As far as I know, Ste. Genevieve has always had a band," says Sam Sexauer, veteran Muny Band member. After returning from World War II, Sexauer recalls gathering with musical cronies at Toad's (now known as the Sandbar). He and his brother Vince recruited other old Knights of Columbus and Lion's Club band members. Their brother, Glennon "Sleepy" Sexauer, Ralph Rodenmeyer, Jack Miller, Cap Donze and Pete Lelie were among the first to form this new marching band. Lelie, who had played with John Philip Sousa's band during the war years, bought instruments and sheet music for the group. By 1946, the new Ste. Genevieve Municipal Band was formed. After practices at the old brewery, brother Vince, who owned the Hotel Ste. Genevieve, would provide a meal of fried chicken and liver dumplings. "I believe it was the food that kept us together in those early days," admits Sexauer. The band led all the patriotic parades, beginning with dirges in the old cemetery and leaving with a snappy Sousa march . "Silver Threads among the Gold" was a standard at wedding anniversaries. "Payment usually amounted to a meal and some beers," he recalled. The Muny Band was fast becoming an integral part of all Ste. Genevieve affairs. In the early 1950s, the town voted in a band tax to pay a stipend to a director and the performers.

Sam recalls his dad's love of music. Ed Sexauer, a plumber by trade and owner of the Palace Bar and City Hotel (now the Hotel Ste. Genevieve), had a passion for music. Each of his nine children played musical instruments and formed their own family band just for fun. Music was contagious in those days. Dance bands were popular in the early and mid-1900s. Among Ste. Genevieve's more famous bands of the twentieth century were the Missouri Ramblers, the Elmo Donze Band, the Jack Trapp Orchestra and the Pat Keifer Band.

Today, the Ste. Genevieve Municipal Band performs its regular summer concert series on Thursday evenings at the Valle schoolyard. A true drive-in concert, patrons line the schoolyard with their vehicles. Many bring lawn chairs or blankets, but some prefer just to listen from their cars. Occasionally, a horn is sounded during the applause following one of the band's numbers. This may at first seem rude to the uninitiated. But a few years ago, when more listeners remained in their cars, honking was the perfectly acceptable form of complimenting the band.

The Forge Band poses at Valle Spring

Even when away from town, Ed Sexauer (third from left in front row) managed to hook up with a band in Guthrie, Oklahoma.

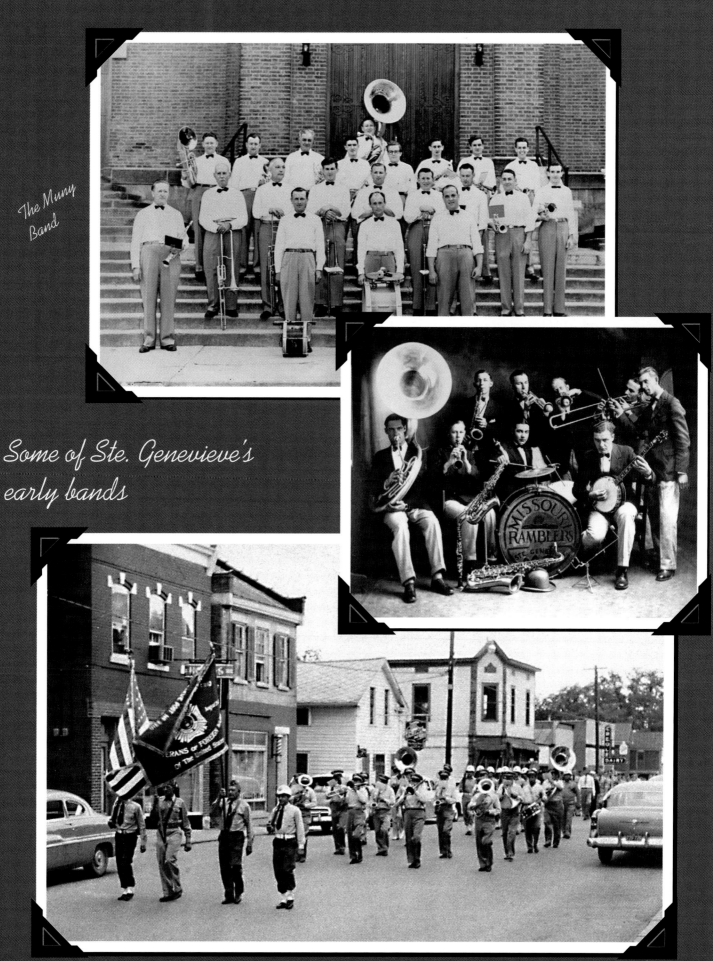

The Muny
Band

Some of Ste. Genevieve's
early bands

The municipal band marches down Market Street at Fourth in a patriotic parade. Notice Bill Sexauer's
tavern and the old Kroger store on the corner. In the background you can see the Creole Dairy sign.

STE. GENEVIEVE'S
Artist Colony

Ste. Genevieve's charm has been an inspiration to countless artistic souls throughout its history. In the 1930s, the town found favor with a group of St. Louis artists who produced numerous works of the old town and its people. Even today, the lines and textures of its buildings provide endless subject matter for artistic studies.

As art came to grips with a number of major changes and challenges during the first decades of the twentieth century, artists' colonies began springing up across the country. Artists sought isolated spots where they could work in a peaceful, yet stimulating environment and feed on the collective energies and inspiration of other kindred spirits.

Ste. Genevieve's rustic charm and quaint solitude lured two St. Louis artists to town—Jesse Beard Rickly and Bernard H. Peters. They founded the Ste. Genevieve Artists' Colony in 1932 and operated out of the historic "Mammy Shaw" House at Merchant and Second.

Aimee Schweig and other top artists from the region, joined the colony. A 1933 *St. Louis Globe-Democrat* article on Rickly and Schweig, explained, "These two women went down from St. Louis because they felt that life there offered an artist something worth preserving."

Young local artist Matthew Ziegler—who offered lodging, food, and hospitality to the group—contributed greatly to the survival of the colony through the years of the Great Depression.

"La Guignolée" a 1942 mural by Martyl Schweig, on the wall inside the Ste. Genevieve Post Office.

"Ste. Genevieve was envisioned as a place of fellowship where—amidst time-hallowed, romantic, and picturesque antiquity—art might be found and created," wrote James Gordon Rogers, Jr. in his 1983 University of Missouri—Columbia masters' thesis, "The Ste. Genevieve Artists' Colony and Summer School of Art." The development of a new, independent Midwestern art tradition was one of the driving forces behind the colony.

A puzzling curiosity at first, the colony was soon warmly embraced by the community. Locals were "unspeakably flattered" when asked to pose for a painting, according to the March 5, 1933 *St. Louis Post-Dispatch.* When the Ste. Genevieve Museum was opened in October, 1933, in anticipation of the 1935 Bicentennial, its grand opening featured a two-person art show by Rickly and Schweig. "It was an honor for the artists' colony and for Rickly and Schweig to have been included in this way," Rogers noted. "Likewise, the show helped to publicize the museum and Ste. Genevieve in St. Louis, and drew many people to the museum."

The artists' colony played a significant role in the emergence of Ste. Genevieve as a tourist destination. The influx of St. Louis and other out-of-town visitors to see the works of Peters,

Local artist Matt Ziegler (1897-1981) at work in his study. A few of Ziegler's works are on display at the Mammy Shaw House (sketched by Roscoe Misselhorn in 1954, opposite page) which headquartered the 1930s Artist Colony.

Rickly, Schweig and others, certainly opened many eyes around the state to the old city's unique charm and appeal.

The early Ste. Genevieve artists were strictly regionalists, riding the tide of popularity regionalism was enjoying in the early 1930s. Missouri's renowned Thomas Hart Benton was at the forefront of the battle, leading the fight against European domination of artistic trends. Later in its life, the colony would embrace regionalism's heated rival, social realism.

"The regionalists were searching more for authentic expressions of traditional American character in their social presentations than they were composing broadsides against the

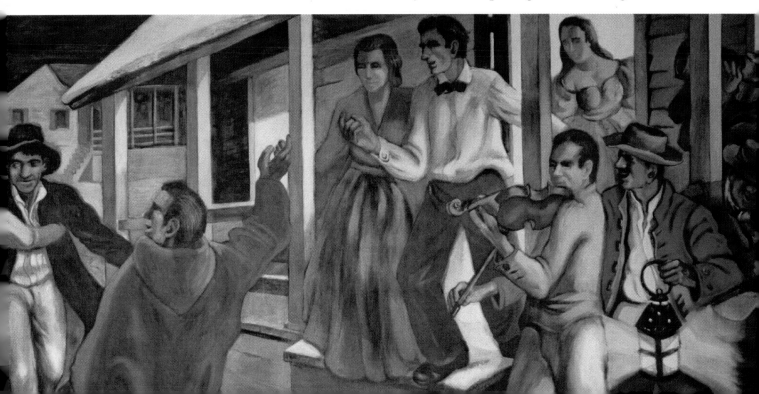

Artist Dolly Surkamp, niece of Matt Ziegler, paints in the garden of the Southern Hotel. "As a child, I thought my uncle's studio was The Art Museum," she recalls of the days of the bustling artist colony.

'establishment,'" Rogers wrote. The continued ravages of the Great Depression would see more and more artists turn to realism.

In 1934, Rickly and Schweig launched the Ste. Genevieve Summer School of Art. The

Guild member Anna Schilli Kirchner at work.

business of overseeing such a school apparently did not set well with the free-spirited Rickly. She left at the end of that year. Schweig took over the school and "outdid herself" in 1936, in Rogers' words, leading to perhaps "the apex of the Ste. Genevieve" experience. That summer Benton and the famed Joe Jones both spoke at the school.

Times were changing, though, and an ugly and protracted strike at Mississippi Lime in 1938—in which Jackson was said to have helped organize the strikers—seemed to leave the old town a bit colder to the artists.

Ziegler, of course, would stay, spending the remainder of his life as Ste. Genevieve's resident artist. He remained in the Shaw House, later adding a studio between it and the Shaw Stone Kitchen (or "Old Indian Trading Post") and briefly tried to revive the art school in the late 1940s. Illinois charcoal artist Roscoe

Misselhorn (an instructor in Ziegler's brief school) would go on to become perhaps the best-loved artist to work in the town.

While the families of the early artists enjoyed visiting Ste. Genevieve (Rogers discovered that Jesse Rickly's husband loved visiting the town's two-lane bowling alley), only one relative of a visiting artist would make her own strides in the field. Martyl Schweig, an impressionable and already hugely talented thirteen-year-old when the colony started, would grow up to leave a lasting artistic legacy in the old town. She won a competition to paint the mural for the new U.S. Post Office, just down the street from the old colony headquarters. Her "La Guignolée," painted in 1942, still graces the Post Office.

Aside from the mural, a few paintings in the city hall, a few scraps of painting paraphernalia unearthed in the Shaw yard by archaeology students in 1998 and an occasional article in an art magazine, the school had largely been forgotten. Relegated to one of the many significant events of the 1930s, it became a mere footnote in the town's history.

The editing and reprinting of Rogers' thesis in book form by The Foundation for Restoration of Ste. Genevieve in 1998 has helped revive the memory of the old colony. So, too, has been the flourishing of the modern Ste. Genevieve Art Guild, formed in the mid-1980s. Once again splendid watercolor and oil paintings and pen and charcoal sketches of historic Ste. Genevieve and its lush landscapes may be seen or purchased. The town which so preoccupied John James Audubon continues to captivate those with artistic souls. —*mle*

Claire Condon and Doris Leffelman enjoy the company of visitors in the shade of a maple at the Felix Valle House.

AL AGNEW

Award-winning wildlife artist Al Agnew signs a print at his gallery in Ste. Genevieve. A native of the eastern Missouri Ozarks, Agnew is an avid outdoorsman whose experiences in the field furnish the material for his paintings. A professional artist since 1983, he has been widely acclaimed for his breathtaking renditions of fur bearing mammals, fish and birds of prey.

AT RIGHT: The lines of distinction between art and craft blur as blacksmith Stan Winkler fashions a piece of steel at his Architectural Ironworks shop.

BELOW: High school and grade school art students have a wealth of subject matter to work from in Ste. Genevieve's historic structures. Here Ron Ohnemus' art class does a study in texture and perspective of the Old Ice House in the 1970s.

Miss 'J'

More than a decade after a debilitating stroke ended Peggy Johnson's coaching career, "Miss J" still casts a huge shadow over Ste. Genevieve sports and the Mineral Area Activities Association her teams once dominated. Peggy Johnson was already in her tenth year as a physical education teacher and volleyball coach at Ste. Genevieve High School in 1973, when the new, challenging game of one-hit volleyball was adopted by the MAAA. Johnson was ready to give it up.

"She was ready to quit," former athletic director Vernon Huck recalled years later. "I was going to help her type the letter." But once Johnson made up her mind to coach the one-hit game—or do anything else—she dove into it and "was always two or three years ahead of other coaches," according to Huck.

Johnson built a true sports dynasty—the school's first. Her teams forged a 277-36-2 record during 13 seasons of one-hit volleyball, including two state championships and two other top four finishes in state. Her teams own nine district championships, ten conference championships and ten MAAA Tournament championships. One of the most amazing feats was her teams' nine-year conference winning streak, from Oct. 14, 1976 to Oct. 21, 1985.

Although Johnson brought the conference its first state championship in any sport (boys or girls) in thirty-five years with her 31-0 team in 1979, her significance in Ste. Genevieve and in female athletics goes well beyond the won-lost records.

Johnson was determination personified. A coach from the "old school," she expected just one thing from her players—one hundred percent effort at all times. Those not meeting her expectations will never forget it.

"It seems like everyone had one good falling out with her," recalled Delores Fleeman Coleman, who played on Johnson's last two teams in 1984 and 1985. "That was all it took. You never wanted to fight with her again."

"She was definitely a disciplinarian," said Theresa Akins Scherer, possibly Johnson's star pupil and leading spiker of the back-to-back state champion teams in 1979 and 1980.

"Her eyes were magic," said Debbie Basler Stolzer, a member of the 15-1 MAAA champion team of 1974. "You never wanted to make a mistake to begin with, but no one's perfect and you did. She'd call that time-out and you'd go in there and you looked at those eyes and it was like magic and you went back out and played your best."

The Warren, Arkansas native expected no less of herself. Despite severe migraine headaches, she consistently stayed up most of the night during volleyball seasons, watching and rewatching opponent game films (another "first" in the area) and scheming offenses and defenses, with magnets on her legendary green magnetic clipboard. Regular substitution and platoon play became an early Johnson trademark. This allowed more girls to contribute. Most of Johnson's innovations were copied by rival coaches.

"How could they not?" Coleman asked. "Everything she did worked. I don't think there was ever anything she told us that didn't work if we did it the way she said."

Johnson's program was significant in another way. Early on, she coined the team nickname "Headhunters." The Ste. Genevieve girls thereby became possibly the first girls' program in Missouri not to be called the "Lady (blank)s" or the (blank)ettes." While some in the community prefer using the seemingly more politically-correct "Hunters" moniker today, those who played against Johnson's dominating teams of the late 1970s and early 1980s believe the traditional nickname was appropriate. During a four-year period, from 1977 through 1980, the Headhunters won 114 games, while losing only five and tying one. They took third place in state once and won two Class 3A state championships.

Johnson not only built the Ste. Genevieve volleyball program into an elite one, she also helped lead female coaches and female sports in general, into a new era of respect. As an early member of the Missouri State Advisory Board for volleyball and girls' track, she became a dominant figure. She was honored by the National Federation of Interscholastic Coaches Association with a "Distinguished Service Award" and the Missouri High School Volleyball Coaches Association now annually presents the Peggy Johnson Excellence in Coaching Award to the state's outstanding coach.

Despite Johnson's legendary toughness, her ex-players remain steadfastly loyal.

"She taught every player she had what respect was," said Tana Thomure Schenck, a member of the 1977 team that went 30-3 and took third place in state. "You respected that lady and that's just the way it was. She was the authority figure and what she said was it."

Mary Alice "Ace" Robertson, a one-time coaching rival, who then served as Johnson's assistant coach (1975-1981), characterized the development of most players' relationship with Johnson. "First dislike; second, fear; third, respect; fourth, tolerance; fifth, like;" she said, "and then I realized at one point that they had all smashed together and grown into love."

Her 1986 stroke left Johnson unable to speak or write. A blow that would have stripped many of hope, however, has not robbed Johnson of hers. Through grueling therapy and countless hours on her own, she has recovered much of her mobility.

Her former players still pick "Miss J" up from time to time and take her to watch them play volleyball.

"Through her dedication in life, she passed on qualities that shine in each of her student athletes," read a plaque her former players presented to her in 1995. "Qualities such as discipline, determination, desire, willpower, success, leadership, having a positive attitude and the pride in being who we are." Later, the certificate added "We'd like to present this token of appreciation to a lady whom we love dearly and have a great deal of respect for. Thank you Ms. Jay, for all the qualities that you've brought out in each of us."

In a community where old-fashioned hard work and character are still considered vital virtues, Johnson helped turn out a generation of women who carry on the same values. "She did push us hard, but at the same time she showed us respect and had faith in us," said Linda Armbruster Roth, a member of the unbeaten 1979 team, who later returned as Johnson's assistant coach. "She had a very special ability to bring out potential in girls who maybe didn't even know they had it. She made weak players into good players; she made good players into exceptional players." —*mle*

The 1966 Valle Warriors

Football powerhouses have become almost passé in Ste. Genevieve. By 1997 Valle Catholic High School had won nine state football championships and Ste. Genevieve High School one. In 1992 Valle won the Class 1A title and Ste. Genevieve the 3A championship. Going undefeated had become almost commonplace at Valle High by the 1990s. One team, however, stands above the fold. The passage of three decades and the mists of legend have begun to make the 1966 Valle Warriors seem more like an elusion than reality.

The 1966 Warriors, though, were real. In a ten-game season (before Missouri introduced football playoffs), the Valle team went 10-0 and outscored its outmanned opponents 535-0. This is no typographical error. Valle outscored opponents by an average of 53.5-0.

"The chances against going unscored on are great," said Ralph Thomure, head football coach at Valle from 1960 through 1973. Thomure, a 1946 Valle graduate, took a leave of absence from his job at McDonnell Aircraft Corporation in 1960 and accepted what was supposed to be a one-year job as football coach. "I was told by Monsignor Edmund Venverloh that my job would probably only be for one year because they were considering dropping football after one more season —unless the team gave a reason that it should remain," Thomure recalled. The team had gone winless in 1959 and had very little equipment on hand.

Thomure's 1960 team went 5-5, though, and revived interest in Valle football. Thomure wound up staying 13 years and went 93-37-2. He is still the winningest coach in Valle football history, not counting playoff games. It was that 1966 season, though, that made the era truly legendary.

"After the third game I knew just being unbeaten was not going to be much of a goal

for them," Thomure said. "The Monday following the third game, we sat on the bleachers and discussed goals. I said it was unlikely they would be beaten this year, but that there was a possibility we could go unscored upon. I said it would be difficult. You can be scored upon in so many different ways. But they all wanted to give it a try."

The numbers were amazing. The Warriors totaled 221 first-downs, to just 42 for the opponent. They gained 4,011 total yards, to 621 for opponents, including a 3,037 to 431 rushing margin. Carl "Foxy" Basler enjoyed what still ranks as possibly the best all-around Warrior season. He ran 165 times for 1,428 yards and an 8.6 average per carry. He scored 25 touchdowns and 154 points.

The Warriors also dominated in the air. Matt Haug, who would go on coach North County and Dexter teams to numerous playoff victories, was the quarterback. Haug completed 54 of 97 passes for 973 yards and threw 17 touchdown passes, against just two interceptions. Valle opponents completed just 22 percent of their passes and were intercepted 22 times by the Warriors.

"An awful lot of people had a shot at carrying the ball. One fact that is often overlooked is that the starters probably only played a little over half the time on offense," Thomure pointed out. "Can you imagine how much they could have scored if they had been in the whole game?"

"I was sometimes accused of running up the score. That's absurd. We tried punting on first down, kicking field goals on first downs—lots of things to try to avoid running up the score."

It didn't work. The Warriors creamed Kinloch 79-0 and Fredericktown 71-0, for two of the biggest routs in school history. In the Fredericktown game nine different players scored for Valle. Seven men scored in the

Kinloch game. Tri-captains of the team were runningback/defensive back Ken Grass, center/linebacker Tom Donze and guard/linebacker Eugene Figge.

Several players went on to play college ball. Basler, who rushed for 356 yards in 24 tries in a 47-0 win over Perryville, played at Missouri Southern. Haug set an Ohio Valley record for passing yardage at Murray State (Ky.) that stood for nearly 20 years. Donze and tackle Glen Arnold played at Southeast Missouri, while end/defensvie tackle and kickoff specialist Dave Ruebsam was on Arkansas State's undefeated NCAA Division II national championship team in 1970. Speedy receiver Clarence "Boo" Meyer, who caught 29 passes for 600 yards and 12 touchdowns, played briefly at Southern Illinois University.

"That kind of effort you only see in people who eventually will be contenders," Thomure reflected. "The faint-hearted tend to die off. They worked very hard and were team-oriented. Many nights I practically had to chase them off the field. They just enjoyed contact and enjoyed working together."

The 1992 team went 14-0 and challenged the 1966 team's scoring record. With an offense led by future Southwest Missouri State quarterback Jeremy Hoog, the Warriors put 531 points on the board, playing four extra games—but gave up 135.

Like Ste. Genevieve's colonial past, the 1966 Warriors have drifted into legend. Fact and myth tend to blur reality. The written record is there, however, for anyone who wishes to look.

The 1966 Valle Warriors were real. —mle

189

Rural Roots

Although there are influences that could take it in a suburban direction, Ste. Genevieve and the surrounding county remain essentially rural in nature. The rolling hills of Ste. Genevieve County are extensively farmed by descendants of the early French, and later, German settlers. As farms have passed from generation to generation, a sense of pride and ownership has protected much of the county from development. Strong opposition by concerned landowners in the Zell area kept a proposed landfill from being realized in the early 1990s.

Some owners are full time farmers. Others moonlight. It is not uncommon for a laborer at Mississippi Lime to come home at the end of the day shift only to hop on his tractor and get in a crop of soybeans before dark.

Their rural roots are reflected in the lifestyles of the inhabitants. Bingo and horseshoes provide the R and Rs here rather then raquetball courts and weightlifting machines. Vacation days are taken from work during turkey and deer hunting season. Quilting is still a popular form of social gathering and a medium for artistic expression. Beautiful handmade quilts are often the grand prize of church and school raffles. Homegrown and canned vegetables find their place not only at the 4-H fair, but also at the farmer's market and on the table at parish picnics. Bake sales continue to be a popular fundraiser for groups. Butchering and sausage-making are still practiced by some.

Part of Ste. Genevieve's characteristic charm comes from its being nestled amidst pristine woodlands and farmlands that have been protected and cared for by generations of its farm families.

Springtime

Crocus, forsythia and Bradford pear followed by redbuds and the fragrant daffodils, tulips and lilacs—Ste. Genevieve awakens from its winter hibernation with garden tours and the springtime French Festival. With or without its festivals, the town, arrayed in its spring beauty, is worth the visit.

Summer

Summer begins in Ste. Genevieve when the Muny Band plays its first concert of the season and the Felix Vallé State Historic Site treats the public to an evening of story telling, gavottes and rondos, lemonade and Madeleines. While the locals are busy with horseshoes, softball and bar-be-ques, tourists view the gardens and museum houses, and visit the many antique/craft shops and restaurants and relax in the fine bed and breakfasts that Ste. Genevieve has to offer. Summer festivals and county parish picnics abound for all to enjoy, and archeological digs are becoming a more common summer event for the academic. The farmer's market offers fresh garden produce, baked goods and lye soap to the early-bird on Saturday mornings.

July Fourth in the Park

With the Mississippi River as a backdrop, the community gathers on the hills of the Père Marquette Park for an evening of patriotic tunes performed by the Municipal Band which is followed by a spectacular fireworks show. The evening concludes with a sparkler display in the outline of the American Flag and the singing of the National Anthem.

County Fair

Whether big tractor pull or little, auctioning the 4H hog, entering the demolition derby or just watching, or chasing the greased pig—there's something for the whole family at the Ste. Genevieve County Fair.

A fearful mob begins to assemble on the town square. Before long, the temper of the crowd has reached fever pitch. They storm the Bastille to release the handful of prisoners. The "Rights of Man" are proclaimed before the assembly. And "Les Petits Chanteurs" lead the crowd in *La Marseillaises*. It happens each July on Bastille weekend.

Losing Your Head
in Ste. Genevieve

Jour de Fête

Since 1966, during the second full weekend in August, quiet little Ste. Genevieve is transformed into a gala gathering of over 600 craftspeople exhibiting their wares to the multitudinous crowds. Plenty of food and entertainment round out the town's largest celebration.

Ste. Genevieve native Walter "Stormy" Crawford, Jr. and "Kuma" –a golden eagle–visit during Jour de Fête. Crawford is founder and executive director of the World Bird Sanctuary headquartered in St. Louis which is one of North America's most respected sanctuaries concerned with the conservation of bird species worldwide.

The wildly colored display of a tie-dyer's craft booth serves as a backdrop to various Jour de Fête scenes.

Project Pioneers

by Betty Valle Gegg

Participants in today's Project Pioneers are celebrating an event that was only an idea ten years ago. The idea was to bring more local participation to the annual Jour de Fête which is held in August of each year. How better than by celebrating families!

Project chairman Lucille Basler recalled a complaint that Jour de Fête doesn't really honor the early families that built Ste. Genevieve. That remark hit home. "Really, except for the few historic buildings which were open to the public, we didn't concentrate on our history and traditions," she reasoned.

After a little brainstorming, a plan was worked out to honor two families each year—one French and one German. The honor would be a family reunion type celebration with family information assembled and available for those who wanted it. The information would come from church records dating from 1759 to 1900. Attendance prizes for the oldest man and oldest lady and those traveling the farthest would be given.

Basler approached the Ste. Genevieve Chamber of Commerce to sponsor the event, not knowing how her proposal would be received.

"They surprised me!" she said. "As soon as I had finished my presentation, someone made a motion to accept the project, a second was given, and everyone said 'aye!' That was the start of Project Pioneers." The celebration has drawn families from as far as Canada and Germany.

The DeGuire-LaRose family and Rottler family were honored the first year in 1989. From then, it was Boyer and Drury in 1990; Aubuchon and Naeger in 1991; Lalumondiere and Joggerst-Jokerst in 1992; Govreau-Govro and Basler in 1993-94; Carron and Gegg in 1995; Papin and Fallert in 1996; Thomure and Flieg in 1997; Valle and Okenfuss in 1998; and Bequette and Huck in 1999.

The Govreau/Govro and Basler families waited an entire year to celebrate. They were to be honored in 1993, but the Great Flood left no time for celebrating—only sandbagging. Over 600 attended that celebration which was postponed until August 1994.

Project Pioneers, in its 10-year span, has spurred much interest in family history. Many are amazed to learn that the neighbor down the street really stems from the same family as they do. In all reality, Project Pioneers has become an interesting chapter in the town's long Jour de Fête history.

Members of the Valle and Okenfuss families visit with historian Lucille Basler during the 1998 Project Pioneers event.

The Zell-Zell Connection
by Betty Valle Gegg

Years ago you could have asked any local resident of German descent where his ancestors were from and he would have answered, "Baden." But today, since the relationship began between Zell-USA and Zell-Weierbach, Germany—Baden is more readily defined as Zell-Weierbach, Fessenbach, Rammersweier, Sasbach or Hofweier, all towns in and near Offenburg, Germany.

A resident of Zell-Weierbach, Max Metzler, is credited with visiting Ste. Genevieve county 14 years ago and noting the common names of the towns of Zell, Weingarten and New Offenburg. He stopped at cemeteries and observed even more common family names here. He took the information back to Mayor Klaus Basler of Zell-Weierbach. Residents of Zell-Weierbach began planning to meet their distant cousins here in Zell, Missouri.

Mayor Basler, his wife and Renee Hauser, an American-born Zell-Weierbach resident, visited here early in 1991 with Zell pastor, Rev. Harold Voekler, to plan the event. Then in September, a group of 60 residents of Zell-Weierbach and the surrounding area arrived and many lasting friendships were forged.

That first visit was a short one with the group gathering at the Hotel Ste. Genevieve for lunch. Some met their host families, while others went with the bus back to the hotel in St. Louis after enjoying the Saturday evening Mass and a dinner and dance at Zell. On Sunday they returned, took part in the Germanfest at Weingarten, then music and dinner at the Zell hall before leaving, teary-eyed, that evening for St. Louis where they continued their tour. It was an emotional parting with the promise to meet again.

One facet of the meeting that has continued to be so meaningful is the German language as it is spoken here by those who

Mayor Klaus Basler of Zell-Weierbach, Germany directs his group in a round of "Abschiedslied" during their 1996 visit to Zell, Missouri and Ste. Genevieve County.

learned it from their parents. In Germany, the language has grown with the times, but local residents here still use the same idioms their ancestors brought with them in the mid-1800s. For our German friends, it is indeed a thrill to hear their language spoken as they recall their ancestors speaking it when they were children.

Since that first visit, cards and letters have kept the communications open. Two years later a group af 50 from Zell and the Ste. Genevieve area visited these newfound friends in Germany. From Friday night through Sunday, many of the local group were guests in German homes, experienced German culture and toured the area that local ancestors once called home.

Every two years since then, there has been a meeting either here or in Germany, and at each event the friendship grows as each learns more about the other's lives and realizes that the differences are less and the commonalities have increased. Perhaps it is in the German descendants of our families that we find such a huge chunk of ourselves, a part that heretofore has been missing.

Autumn

School has begun and along with it a flurry of activity. Soccer and football players and cross country runners mingle with the changing vista. In the fields, corn and soybeans are being harvested and the color of goldenrod, purple and white asters and the tall bright yellow daisied Jerusalem arti-chokes glow at the fence rows in the warm seasonal light. Soon the sassafras will begin the autumnal display with its bright tips of red. Shopkeepers dress their shops in the colors of the season with chrysan-themums, cornstalks and pumpkins, ghosts and jack-o-lanterns. The Saturday morning farmer's market features apples, gourds, pumpkins and Indian corn. Besides the county's many parish German fests and beer gardens, the little French village of Ste. Genevieve celebrates with an October harvest fest of its own. The German Band, Schuhplattler Dancers, bratwurst and beer, and a hot air balloon lift-off are just a few of the

attractions. *Les Petits Chanteurs become "Die Kleine Singers" for two days entertaining with such rousing Deutsch favorites as* Ach du Lieber Augustin *and* Freut Euch Des Lebens. *Valle and Ste. Gen. alumni flock home to watch the homecoming parades and games. The homecoming queen, in her sleeveless dress which was purchased in the heat of September, now shivers in the October chill as she is crowned by the retiring queen at half-time. Autumn is not over for the football title town until another state championship is decided.*

Winter

*A*t no other season is the quiet little town transformed so much as with the first snowfall of winter. Then the streets are hushed and the lights of street lamps sparkle off the fresh blanket of snow. One can walk the silent streets and imagine themselves in the French colonial village of the late 1700s.

The holidays begin with the festive Christmas Walk parade on the first weekend in December. Shops give samples of hot cider and cookies to visitors and strolling carolers. The annual Christmas tree lighting brings locals and visitors together for the singing of seasonal songs. The warm glow of candle-light transforms tour homes to any earlier time before electricity. The Presbyterian youth group braves the elements as they portray the live nativity scene.

The festival's final event is a Christmas concert performed in the Church of Ste. Genevieve. Although the church is dressed only in its solemn Advent purple, the music of the bell ringers draws the crowds inside to listen and reflect on the season and the beauty of the Gothic church and to hear the joy-inspiring Ste. Genevieve Wind Ensemble and Community Choir.

A French Christmas

The birth of Jesus remains the focus of the season for Christians in Ste. Genevieve. Church youth groups re-enact the nativity during special church services. At the Felix Vallé State Historic Site the table is set for a traditional French colonial Christmas in December complete with elaborate food and decorations, all containing some Christian symbolism. The crèche—French nativity scene—is displayed as the focal point and tour guides explain how the French children would add new characters to the scene each day of Advent until on Christmas eve the Christ child would be laid in the manger.

The same thing, though not a re-enactment, happens in Ste. Genevieve's Catholic Church. Though the secular world outside may be decorated and already feasting, the solumn purple of Advent, the stark Giving Tree and the incomplete nativity scene are the only decor until Christmas eve. On that joyous eve, the candles are lit and the church is adorned with poinsettias, beautifully decorated Christmas trees, and gold and white trim and greenery. The Christ child is laid in the manger and the French carols are sung during midnight Mass. Children fall asleep during the incantation and perhaps remain so until they are tucked in ther beds. For many, Midnight Mass marks the beginning of

the twelve days of Christmas and just as the colonial French had their réveillon, a feast of bouillon, pralines and divinité await Ste. Genevieve contemporaries as they arrive home from the midnight services.

Appendix A

On Photo Retouching
"Let the Viewer Beware"

BEFORE RETOUCHING

AFTER RETOUCHING—Poles and lines removed

We hope you've enjoyed your leisurely stroll through Ste. Genevieve. If, after browsing the pages of this book, you've come away with a sense of the personality of Ste. Genevieve, then we've accomplished what we set out to do. As you have seen, the book is not a detailed chronology of the history of the town, but rather a cross-section of this historic little community.

To the extent that this book is ever used as a source of historical documentation, we've attempted to be as accurate as current information will allow, regarding facts and dates. However, we feel an obligation to make the reader aware of some license which has been taken regarding the pictorial information in the book.

It used to be that photographs were a fairly reliable source of historical information. One could determine, for instance, the vintage of a photograph based on the style of clothing that people in the picture were wearing or other details such as license plates, signs, etc.

Today, however, modern technology, in the hands of a skilled artist, allows photographic manipulation to the extent that even the most trained eye cannot detect whether an image has been tampered with. All of the old darkroom tricks once practiced by darkroom technicians to enhance and alter a photograph are now possible using powerful computer programs to accomplish the same end.

We have taken advantage of that technology in preparing the 562 images of this book for printing. When appropriate, we have retouched or restored a photograph, but only to the degree to make it more pleasing visually. For instance, some photos of Ste. Genevieve's historic houses were retouched to remove power lines and utility poles which detract from the composition. In other cases, cracks and scratches were removed from some of the vintage photos in the book.

In any case, manipulation of the photos has been done only to accomplish a more aesthetically pleasing image. We hope the historical purist can forgive the liberties we've taken in preparing the images for this book. No attempt was made to deceive the viewer. —*bn*

Two seperate camera plates in the archives of the Ste. Genevieve Museum show the first train arriving in Ste. Genevieve on June 11, 1899. We spliced the two together to create the dynamic panorama on pages 22 and 23.

AT LEFT: *The best angle of the Guibourd-Vallé House is this view of both its eastern front and southern side, but a utility pole dissects the composition. BELOW: With the pole removed through retouching, the visual impact of the portrait of the house is restored.*

What color dresses were Betty Donze and Vera Okenfuss wearing at the time of this photograph? We'll never know—this image, as well as all of those in the composite on page 170, started out as black and white. They were hand-tinted in the computer to enhance the composition. By the way, Bill's Photo Lab in Ste. Genevieve does an excellent job of photo restoration and compositing.

Sometimes false assumptions are made about a photograph even when it hasn't been manipulated. This image of the old Merchant's Bank (a.k.a. The Rottler Building) which once stood on the SW corner of Main and Merchant Streets might be mistaken for the Palace Bar due to the sign in the foreground. It so happens that the sign of the Palace Bar, which once operated out of the City Hotel (now Hotel Ste. Genevieve) located across the street (photo above), shows up in the photograph and appears to be affixed to the Rottler Building.

This photograph leads one to assume that modern tugs and barges (seen in the background) were in operation on the river at the same time as the Ste. Genevieve Transfer Ferry. What we're seeing, in fact, is a photo of a scale model of the ferry by Lewis Pruneau photographed at Little Rock Landing with the Mississippi as a backdrop. The model is on display at the Ste. Genevieve Museum.

Although a view camera and wide-angle lens could accomplish the same effect, it was just as easy to distort the Old Academy in the computer to give its eerie appearance on page 92.

Bibliography

Basler, Lucille, *Church of Ste. Genevieve,* Ste. Genevieve, Wehmeyer Printing Co.

Brackenridge, Henry Marie, *Recollections of the Persons and Places in the West,* Philadelphia: J.B. Lippincott & Co., 1868.

Douglass, Robert S., *History of Southeast Missouri,* New York: Lewis Publishing Co., 1912

Duckett, Leola Amoureux, *The Amoureux Family in Ste. Genevieve,* 1985.

Ekberg, Carl J., *Colonial Ste.Genevieve,* Tuscon:The Patrice Press, 1996

Ellis, Gerald W., *A Study of Kaskaskia, Illinois*

Franzwa, Gregory M., *The Story of Old Ste. Genevieve,* St. Louis: The Patrice Press, 1990.

Franzwa, Gregory M., *The Oregon Trail, Rediscovered: Silver Anniversary Edition,* Tuscon: The Patrice Press, 1997

Gould's St. Louis Directory, St. Louis: 1871, 1873, 1877, 1879, 1881, 1886, 1888, 1889, 1893, 1896, 1897, 1900, 1902, 1904, 1909, 1910, 1911, 1913, 1915, 1925, 1926.

Guibourd, Omar, diary, *Missouri Historical Society Bulletin Vol. VIII:* St. Louis, 1952.

Guyette, Richard P., *Tree Ring Dating of French Colonial Vertical Log Houses in Ste. Genevieve, Missouri,* Columbia: the University of Missouri-Columbia, 1985.

_____, *Wood Use in French Colonial Vertical Log Houses in Ste. Genevieve, Missouri,* Columbia: the University of Missouri-Columbia, 1985.

Guyette, Richard P. and Overby, Osmund, "The first tree ring dating of a building in Missouri," *Missouri Preservation News,* Fall, 1984.

History of Southeast Missouri, Chicago: The Goodspeed Publishing Co., 1888.

Luer, Jack R. and Francis, Jesse W., *The Vanishing French Heritage,* 1999

Overby, Osmund, *Historic American Buildings Survey,* HABS No. MO-1109, Columbia: 1987

_____, *Ste. Genevieve Architectural Survey,* Columbia: University of Missouri-Columbia, 1985.

Peterson, Charles E., "A Guide to Ste. Genevieve, with Notes on its Architecture," National Park Service, 1939.

Petrequin, Harry J., *Stories of Old Ste. Genevieve:* Cape Girardeau, 1934.

Rogers, James Gordon, Jr., *The Ste. Genevieve Artists' Colony and Summer School of Art,* University of Missouri-Columbia, 1983

Sharp, Mary Rozier and Sharp, Louis J., III, *Between the Gabouri.* Ste. Genevieve: Histoire de Rozier, 1981.

Siler, Jacob, *Siler's Historic Photos: Volume I, Number I,* St. Louis: 1904.

Ste. Genevieve *Fair Play,* various issues from 1880, 1885, 1886, 1897, 1930, 1935, 1939, 1949 and 1957.

Ste. Genevieve *Herald,* various issues from 1884, 1885; 1897, 1909, 1911, 1912, 1930, 1935.

Williams, Rick and Gegg, Betty Valle, *"We Can Do This!" Fighting the Flood of 1993,* Ste. Genevieve Herald, 1993

Thurman, Melburn D., *Building A House in 18th Century Ste. Genevieve,* Ste. Genevieve: Pendragon's Press, 1984.

Personal Communication
Jim Baker, 1997, 1998
Fran Ballinger, 1997
Lucille Basler, 1997, 1998
Timothy G. Conley, 1996, 1997
Ernest Allen Connally, 1997
Carl J. Ekberg, 1996, 1997, 1998
Susan Flader, 1997
Gregory M. Franzwa, 1997, 1998
Richard P. Guyette, 1997
Jack Luer, 1997
Frank Myers, 1997
Osmund Overby, 1997, 1998
Arthur Papin, 1999
Charles E. Peterson, 1997, 1998
Carl Shinabarger, 1997, 1998
Lorraine Stange, 1997, 1998
Bonnie Stepenoff, 1998
Kit Wesler, 1997

Other Reading
Legacies of a French Empire in North America by Véronique Deplanne, Donning Company Publishers,1999

Index